The Shattering of the Great
Planets
Hesperus and Phaethon

Second Edition
Published by METRON PUBLICATIONS
P.O. Box 1213
PRINCETON NJ 08542-1213
USA
METRONAX
B.P. 60062
72403 LA FERTE BERNARD CEDEX
FRANCE
ISBN # 978-1-60377-078-1
Library of Congress Control Number: 2009923746

Johann Gottlieb Radlof

The Shattering of the Great Planets Hesperus and Phaethon

and the Ensuing Destructions and Floods on Earth;

with new considerations about the myth-language of the Ancient Peoples.

translated from the German by
Anne-Marie de Grazia

First published in Berlin, 1823

Table of Contents

Foreword: A Note about the Author

PART ONE :

Image-Language and Myths of Ancient Peoples.

Chapter 1.: Protohistoric Myths.

Chapter 2.: Protohistoric Myths:Their Content.

Chapter 3.: Image-language and Image-writing.

Chapter 4.: Representation of Greek visual artists and poets.

Chapter 5.: Visual representation of particular actions and events.

Chapter 6.: Lost representations of visual artists.

Chapter 7.: Secret image language of the Apocalypse.

Chapter 8.: Obscured knowledge resulting in erroneous explanation of visual art and imaged tales through the latter Greeks.

Chapter 9.: Erroneous interpretation of myths by the modern.

PART TWO :

The Change of Orbit of Planet Hesperus and the Ensuing Floods

Chapter 1.: Displacement of Planet Hesperus.

Chapter 2.: Collision with other heavenly bodies, as the cause of this event.

Chapter 3.: The Ogygian Flood and its place in time.

Chapter 4.: Earlier deluges in the time of Noah and Xisuthros.

Chapter 5.: Fiery eruptions, new islands and loss of Atlantis.

Chapter 6.: The Inachian Flood.

Chapter 7.: Thessalian or Deucalion Flood - its extension.

Chapter 8.: Accompanying natural events.

Chapter 9.: Fixing the date of the Flood.

PART THREE :

The Shattering of Planet Hesperus.

Chapter 1.: Phaethon, at first a planet between Mars and Jupiter.

Chapter 2.: Traces of a residual knowledge in the names of the neighboring planets.

Chapter 3.: Ovid's image-tale of Phaethon.

Chapter 4.: Explanatory remarks.

Chapter 5.: Continuation. Wanderings of the Ligurians towards the North.

Chapter 6.: Image tales of this and other heavenly occurrences in Nonnus.

Chapter 7.: The image-tale in Hyginus, Hesiod and Servius.

Chapter 8.: Remarks about the date of this event.

Chapter 9.: Eridanus in Prussia.

Chapter 10.: Boreas and the Eumolpides: the Eridanus in Heaven.

Chapter 11.: Origin and meaning of the name Eridanus.

Chapter 12.: Origin of amber according to the myths of the nordic peoples.

Chapter 13.: High value of amber; Elektra walking back towards the North.

Chapter 14.: Names of amber and their origins.

Chapter 15.: Many erroneous explanations of the image-tale of Phaethon.

PART FOUR :

Later events and natural events until the year 1440 BC.

Chapter 1.: Exceptional human migrations since the Great Floods.

Chapter 2.: The last flood under the reign of Dardanus, and the fire on Mount Ida.

Chapter 3.: Comets and the piling up of mountains of water.

Chapter 4.: The Giant Typhoeus and his comet.

Chapter 5.: The devastations of Typhoeus on Earth.

Chapter 6.: His fight against Jupiter and the comet.

Chapter 7.: Additional remarks, and information about Typheus from other writings.

PART FIVE AND LAST :

Looking Back on the Events Aforementioned

Chapter 1.: Twice a change of the Earth axis.

Chapter 2.: Atmospheric transformations on our earth.

Foreword:

A Note About the Author

Johann Gottlieb Radlof, a German philologist whose merits were recognized by Jacob Grimm, Friedrich Hegel, Friedrich Schlegel and the poet Jean-Paul, was born in Merseburg, in Saxony-Anhalt, in 1775 and died, date and place unknown, probably sometime shortly after 1826, having produced a considerable amount of work in the study of German dialectic languages, a field in which he was a pioneer. In one of his early works, he collected and compared versions of two parables of the Bible in a large variety of German dialects. Not much is known about him, except that he seems to have had extraordinary bad luck, and an extraordinarily difficult character. He no doubt was an original mind, a scholar endowed with an awesome pedantic knowledge while in the same time capable of bold ideas, sometimes to the point of weirdness... He worked with Campe on one of the important early dictionaries of the German language and broke with him after letter 'A.' He was a "pain in the neck," with a nationalistic bend and sense of mission ("to save and tend the Germanic wonder-tree whose tap- root is grounded in the soil of Persia and India"). At age 28,

he wrote to Goethe and Schiller, enlightening them about
the possibilities of old southern German languages to
enrich the modern language. He crusaded for the use of
the absolute genitive and against diphtongues. He
addressed Goethe again in 1816, vituperating about the
appalling spelling used by the delegates to the Congress
of Vienna, after the Napoleonic Wars. A few years later,
he published a "Comprehensive Treatise" on German
spelling "for the use of Thinkers, especially Writers,
Teachers and Public Servants," dedicating no less than
forty pages to "fricative and sibilant sounds..." His
philological insights have sometimes been recognized as
brilliant, and despite having written a lost diatribe against
"The Tyranny of French Language and Thought holding
sway over Europe since the Peace of Rastadt," he
conceived of his own role as a grammarian rather in the
way of the French Academy, as an intransigeant last
instance lawgiver in matters of language, in contrast with
the descriptive scientific approach imposed by the
brothers Grimm. His knowledge of the ancient sources,
Greek and Latin, accessible in his time is unexcelled. It
comes to the fore in *The Shattering of the great Planets
Hesperus and Phaethon and the ensuing Destructions and Floods
on Earth; with new Considerations about the Myth-Language of
the Ancient Peoples,* published in 1823 where, no
astronomer himself and not pretending to be, he grabs at
the hypothesis of the break-up of a planet between the

orbits of Mars and Jupiter, which had been posited by astronomers one generation earlier to explain the origin of the asteroid belt, and links it with the ancient myth of Phaethon and the numerous flood-histories, using exclusively the knowledge transmitted from ancient texts, with remarkable rigor, and makes a breathtaking attempt at dating these events. He presents his credentials as: "Doctor and Professor, Correspondent and Effective Member of the Royal Bavarian Academy of Sciences in Munich, of the German Society in Berlin, as well as member of the Cameralistic Society of Erlangen."

Part One:

Image-Language and Myths of Ancient Peoples.

Chapter One

Protohistoric Myths.

Were one to raise the question among the moderns: "But what, in the end, are the ancient peoples trying to tell us about the ages preceding history - that is, the time before their own prosaic history developed - concerning the prevailing environmental conditions, and events which occurred during the time leading back from their own present to their earliest origins?" - we would receive varied answers, depending on the peoples considered. "The Hebrews," one would have said not so long ago, "instruct us by the means of divine revelation about the time of Creation all the way down to their own times," whereas presently, at least as concerns the earliest periods of their history, we would grant to them merely the handing down of legends and traditions. "The

Assyrians," it is asserted, "offer us, up to the time of the creation of their empire by Ninus,[1] and according to their own and to Jewish chronicles, but the debris of a history; whereas the Egyptians, in their priestly chronicles from the times of Psammetich[2] up to those of Menes,[3] bring us mere historical affabulations, which their chronology, reaching several thousand years beyond Moses, makes appear even more fanciful; as for the Indians, before Alexander's irruption into their lands, they contribute only romantic epics and god-fables; the Greeks, lastly, before the flourishing of their prosaic historians Herodotus and Pherekides,[4] also provide us, all the way to the Trojan war, merely with heroic romances, as well, of course, as with grandiose allegories, such as those of

---

[1] Founder of Nineveh, husband of Semiramis. His reign supposedly lasted 52 years, beginning in 2189 BC, according to Ctesias, a Greek historian of the 4th century BC.

[2] Pharaoh of the Twenty-Sixth Dynasty of Egypt (595 BC - 589 BC).

[3] Pharaoh of the First Dynasty, the founder or second of this dynasty. Dates ca. 3100 BC - 3000 BC. Herodotus refers to him as Min. According to Manetho, he reigned 62 years and was killed by a hippopotamus.

[4] Greek philosopher of the VI. century BC. Born on Syros. Teacher of Pythagoras. Only a few fragments of his work survive.

Homer; but as one moves upwards from there, and up to the origins of the peoples, we encounter a mere chaos of myths, purporting to report the story of the ancestors and of the gods, but which in reality are only "philosophemes," that is, elaborations upon speculations about the origins of the world and of human beings."

Must we believe, therefore, that the numerous, painstakingly elaborated chronicles of the colleges of Egyptian priests merit less our trust than those of Moses, who drew his own scant knowledge from no other place than these chronicles themselves, and who possibly was forced to leave behind the books of sacred scriptures which he had carried with him on his exodus from Egypt? Or that men filled out the long ages which stretched between their origins and the beginning of the historical record merely with divine otioseness and romantic dreams? Or that tirelessly active Nature went into a long slumber and provided them with no memorable material through one or another of her mighty transformations? Or that the enticing representations of the most ancient peoples, adorned with all the magic and charms of poetic language, must not contain a true history, for the simple fact that they do not present themselves in the mediocre attire of everyday prose? Or that the peoples themselves could have possibly stepped onto the stage of earliest knowledge and culture in any other guise than richly clad in images and poetic adornments? These are all-important questions,

which we will only be able to answer satisfyingly once we
have paid special attention to the language itself, in which
the so-called myths and allegories have been carried
down to us in their earliest written forms.

Chapter Two

Protohistoric myths: their content.

If we now set ourselves to examining the edifice of the oldest traditions, known under the vocable of *Ur-legends* (i.e. myths), we by and large do not find in them any set of propositions about any single subject of knowledge, but in the contrary, they give us a "whole picture," i.e. they offer us the holistic set of knowledge of the peoples of those times, concerning God, nature, the origin of things, the history of the people itself and of their ancestors, and this, whether the people in question be constituted by one single element (or else stemming from a congregation of many elements into some large single unit), as was the case for instance of the old-Indian, or the Hebrew tribes, which presented a self contained unity; or whether it be constituted by migrants from many other peoples, congregating from all the points of the compass, as was the case of the Greeks; this "whole picture" appears all too often as a tissue of contradictory information, into which only later art and science attempted to bring the necessary consistency. Only when the peoples reach a later cultural stage, when prose writing separates itself from poetry, does this chaotic knowledge divide itself into separate fields, such as history, poetry, natural sciences, etc, each one of which, from that point on, develops on its own.

The old issue, whether man walked out of the hand of the Creator spiritually and morally perfect, and only faltered through the misuse of his freedom; or whether he was created imperfect and grossly sensual and needed to work himself, amid constant fighting and setbacks, into a state of spiritual, intellectual and moral perfection, has no bearing on the considerations above, and, through the myths which have come down to us, the ancient peoples do not appear to us either as spiritually perfect ideals, nor as being morally defective; but, if anything, as human beings much alike those we find in various epochs and places, down to this day.

Chapter Three

Image-language and image-writing

The oldest script of most peoples, for instance of the Egyptians, as well as the Mexicans,' was a picture-script, i.e. one which depicted the objects which were apprehended by the senses with a sensually apprehensible symbol, and those not apprehended by the senses with symbols of such apprehensible physical objects in which the qualities of the non-physical were purported to be contained - for instance, prudence was represented by an eye, the idea of intelligence was transmitted by a snake. In this, it followed the steps of language itself, which in its first beginnings designated abstractions in just such a sensory way, so that with many primitive peoples today we do not meet with any abstract words.

Yet as soon as human beings attain scientific knowledge, they exchange the physical images in language and script for less apprehensible ones. But orators, poets and especially visual artists, who must primarily wreak their effect on the senses, preserve for themselves the usage of the old picture language. So that, for instance, Moses, the lawgiver, in order to wean the Hebrews from the common sensual polytheism of the normal Egyptians and to bring them to the unique deity of the chosen people, forbade them all representation of the Highest Being in any image or sensual form - yet this same Being continues in Moses own words to fly on the wings of the wind, or in Ezechiel, to drive in the carriage of thunder, led on by cherubim and celestial emblematic beasts; in short, in the writings of the Old Testament, this Eternal Being speaks -- talks, vituperates, gets angry, loves, hates and punishes entirely in a human way, if in an exalted form.

This anthropomorphism reigns still in the more modern, fully de-sensualized expression, indeed even in the preaching and chants of those contemporary communities of the Faith which otherwise attempt to replace all sensual and imaged designation of the Eternal through such that are deprived of all sensuality. It is to no effect and futile to attempt to ban all artistry and sensual representation, yet it is also debasing to the divine to drown it in the sensual altogether: it is only through a combination of both approaches that a fitting effect can be gained.

Chapter Four

Representation of Greek visual artists and poets.

Among all the poets of Antiquity, it is the Greeks who have preserved for us the greatest number of remnants of the old Egyptian hieroglyphic script, albeit in a much beautified form. Their representations are in fact almost all of a plastic nature, i.e. they are so thoroughly animated by living, sense-endowed being, that they could just as well have been created by a visual artist. Homer, for one, transfigures the passions which move the heart of men - mighty love, quarrelsome hatred, etc., into goddesses, Aphrodite, Eris, which appear among men as co-actors; he shows wise thought, prudent foresight as sublime Minerva (Athene), who stands by his heroes through danger, and who, in the form of a young shepherd, advises the shipwrecked Ulysses, himself in the disguise of a beggar, to push ahead to the royal palace and there, before any other undertaking, to gather intelligence about the situation of his wife Penelope. "Among the original representations," says Varro, "there is one designating heaven, another the earth, yet another the original form of things, called 'idea' by Plato: Jupiter, as

it were, being the heavens, Juno earth, and Minerva
ideas; further, the heaven is that which creates, the
earth the matter over which it works, as well as the
original form after which something is created." [5] In
other places this historian, to whom the idea of an
Eternal Being was not foreign, explains many of the
divinities of his time as mere sensualisations of
unbodily objects, but yet many more - in agreement
with Polybius, Strabo, Diodorus and other thinkers, as
real human beings who, because of their spiritual
powers, strength, or important inventions were deified
by lesser mortals, whose gratitude they had thus
ensured themselves. A few old-Egyptian imaged
stories, like the beautiful symbolism of animal lust
represented through a serpent, by which Eve is
seduced into tasting the apple, are known to us from
the writings of the Old Testament.

But the language of the visual artist, i.e. the
sculptor, image-maker and painter, is much more
limited than that of the poet, indeed, far more limited
than any language of sounds; for it cannot address itself
by way of the ear to the infinite realm of sounds, but

---

[5] Varro, 116-27 BC, *fragment.* "In simulacris aliud
significare caelum, aliud terram, alied exempla rerum, quas
Plato appellat ideas; caelum, Jovem; terram, Junonem;
ideas, Minervam intelligi; caelum, a quo fit aliud; terram, de
qua fit; exemplum, secundum quod fiat."

only to the eye, therefore, it can convey its message only by means of form and position. The great realm of non-sensual transformations, all abstractions, are therefore excluded from the representations of the visual arts, except insofar as the transformations and de-sensualisations can be hinted at. Therefore, if de-sensualized objects, or full-length tales needed to be represented, it was necessary to first translate them into the language of tales, i.e. they had to be transformed into images and living beings. If we consider the Greek myths, we discover that a considerable number of them consist in such translations from the non-sensual or the lesser-sensual language, into the language of the visual artist, and that therefore those myths, as they were told by poets and priests, prove to be congruent with the representations of the visual artists.

Chapter Five

Visual representation of particular actions and events.

Greek myths and visual artworks furnish us with numerous examples for the preceding propositions. For instance, according to Diodorus,[6] in ancient times the Nile, named then on account of its tearing speed "the eagle," ('Aetos'), had broken through all the dams of Egypt, and had especially laid waste the governorship of Prometheus, so that the latter was tempted to take his own life in despair; but Hercules with his army stopped the rupture and led the stream back into its old bed. Visual artists then would have represented Hercules as he is killing the eagle who eats at the liver of the shackled Prometheus. Moreover, according to the same author,[7] the Greek Hercules had deviated the river Achelous, which had swamped all land around it, had dammed it up and in so doing, had gained a large portion of fertile land for cultivation. In

---

[6] Diodorus Siculus (ca 90 BC - ca 30 BC), Greek historian, born at Argyrium, Sicily. His history, *Bibliotheca historia*, consists of forty books; *Bibliotheca historia*, Book I,

[7] Diodorus Siculus, *Bibliotheca historia*, Book IV,

order to transmit the memory of these events, sculptors fashioned a bull of gigantic size, named Achelous, which Herkules vanquished in battle. During the battle, he broke off one of its horns, the horn of Amalthea, out of which now the overflow exited. At any rate, in visual representations, according to Claudius Aelianus[8], rivers were shown either in the shape of a bull, or of a human being; according to their nature, it could take the form of a man with horns, of a woman, or of a young boy; floods and inundations were represented by water snakes, i.e. through Python, whom Apollo killed with his arrow in front of Delphi, and through the Hydra of Lerna, whose continually sprouting heads Hercules cut off in one fell swoop. Maybe that the artists meant to represent through the sea-serpent, who enfolded in its coils the sacrificing Laokoon and his children by the seaside, only a sudden flood, in which they had found their death; in Quintus Galaber,[9] those

---

[8] Claudius Aelianus (c.175 AD - c. 235 AD), Roman author and rethorician, born at Praeneste, flourished under Septimus Severus and Elagabalus; *Varia Historia*, Book II., *33*.

[9] Quintus Smyrnaeus, or Quintus Galaber (or Calaber), latter part of the 4th century AD, some ascribe him to the 3th century AD, or even earlier. He wrote a following to the Iliad, known as *Posthomerica*. He was known to ancient byzantine writers, but the only known manuscript of his work was discovered in 1450 in Otranto, Puglia, by Cardinal Bessarion; *Posthomerica*, v.443.

serpents belong to the race of Typhon, and he has them preceded by earthquakes.

As Hercules had marched through Africa with a large army, in order to fight against Geryon[10] in Erytheia, one artist got the assignment to represent the difficulties which met the hero in crossing the Atlas mountain range. To this effect, he fashioned a giant, Antaeus (the adversary) who, as long as he was in contact with the earth, remained invincible, for, being his mother, she fed him constantly with new strength. Herkules then lifted him from the ground and strangled him.

King Geryon's domination over three countries was represented by the ancients in figures with three bodies, or three heads; also Kekrops, who moved from Egypt into Attica, was represented in images as two-bodied, which was interpreted by the later Greeks to mean "two-landed," or bi-lingual - of two lands, or of two languages. - The death of Niobe and of her children, i.e., of her peoples, through the plague, was eternalized by the Greek artists through magnificent representations, which show Apollo's arrows hitting the children, while the mother is petrified, unceasing

---

[10] Geryon, a Titan who dwelled on the island of Erytheia of the Hesperides, to the Western extremity of the Mediterranean. Hesiod, Stesichorus and Strabo all point to the region of Cadiz, in Southern Spain, as being Erytheia.

tears flowing from the stone she has been turned into. As their delicacy forbade them to represent anything that provoked disgust or offense, they were not allowed to show the abcesses of the plague, only the killing by the arrows of the invisible Sun God. Homer too attributes the plague in the Greek camp to the arrows of Apollo. These symbolic representations of the ancients situate themselves, in relation to the merely descriptive treatment of specific events by the moderns, as poetry relates to newspaper prose, and captivate the reflective spectator with a far mightier thrill.

Chapter Six

Lost representations of visual artists.

Yet many representations by visual artists have obviously ended up on a wrong path, as for instance the famous representations of the centaurs. The oldest tales report in fact: "Hercules vanquished Tauriskus and Geryon," and many comments point to Tauriskus having reigned within the alpine area. It is known that the Taurisci lived next to the Genni; they were both Celtic or Germanic peoples; the name of the first is connected to the word *Tauern,* which up to this day in Carniola,[11] Styria and Tyrol, designates a high unfertile mountain, as opposed to the *"Alp,"* which means a mountain with pastures. The most ancient poets name several centaurs - i.e. king-rulers reigning over these mountain areas - but nowhere do they mention that these would have been beings made-up as half bull *(tauros)* and half man; still they mention that the daughter of one of them was named Hippa, mare. It is only with the later poets, who probably had preserved little knowledge of the true events, that we encounter the evolving fable, that those giants were half bull, half

---

[11] in Slovenian, *Kranjska,* a region of Slovenia.

man; and in the visual arts, who were not enticed by the idea of a bull shape as the completion of the perfect human form, we find the celebrated representation of humans whose lower body is that of a horse. From then on, the poets joined with the sculptors in further adapting this version by creating a fable of their own. According to this legend, Theseus attempted to abduct Proserpina, daughter of the Molossian king Aïdoneus, for the benefit of his friend Pirithous. The attempt failed, Pirithous was murdered, Theseus was made a prisoner and freed only after a long time by Hercules. Misled by the similarity in names, later artists and poets went to work representing these heroes in the act of trying to abduct the Queen of the Underworld, wife of Pluto. These manners of erroneous representations occur not uncommonly in the history of Greek myths.

Chapter Seven

Secret image language of the Apocalypse.

Among the imaged and symbolic representations from
Christian antiquity, the message of Saint John
distinguishes itself especially by its beauty and audacity,
despite the fact that the innumerable attempts at
explanations on the part of the ancients as well as of
the modern were mostly doomed to failure through
sheer ignorance of the key, which the apostle suggested
to the Seven Communities of Asia Minor as having
been agreed upon in concert. Yet this key is hinted at
with sufficient precision through the whole context,
through the inner coherence of the writing, as well as
through the historical conditions which prevailed at the
time. For then the Romans, dominating the world,
wallowing in crimes and vices, aspired to drag all the
better peoples of the Earth into slavery and immorality,
and therefore persecuted the disciples of the pure
Christian doctrine, which threatened doom to its
polytheism, with the cruelest of martyrdom, and
declared as criminal all free enquiries of thinkers into

the sciences and arts,[12] so that even the historical works, which still held the promise of truth, were mutilated and burned on the forum.[13] Then it happened that all the noble thinkers were forced either to retire into obscurity, or, as was the case with Tacitus, to try to hide the truth from the powers of repression by means of a repressed representation. The exalted prophet John, in order not to be understood by the non-initiated, chose for his messages, in which he gave solace to the Seven Communities and informed them of the conditions then prevailing, as well as of the

---

[12] Pliny the Younger (63 AD -113 AD), Gaius Plinius Cecilius Secundus, lawyer, author and natural philosopher of ancient Rome, nephew and heir of Pliny the Elder. He is known chiefly for his magnificent collection of letters, *Epistulae; Epistulae,* III., *5:* Dubi ifermonis octo (libros) scripsit (avunvulus) sub Nerone, novistimis anniis, quum omne studiorum genus laullo liberius et erectius periculosum servitus periculosum feciset.

[13] Tacitus (56 AD -117 AD), Publius Cornelius, major Roman historian, author of *The Histories, The Annals* and other works; *Agricola (De Vita et Moribus Iulii Agricolae), c. 2:* Legimus, cum Aruleno Rustico Paetus Thrasea, Herennio Senecioni Priscus Helvidius laudati essent, paitale fuisse: neque in ipsos modo auctores, sed in libros quoque eorum saevitum, delegato triumviris ministerio, ut monumenta clarisfimorum ingeniorum in comitio ac foro urerentur. Scilicet, illo igne vocem Populi Romani et libertatem Senatus, et conscientiam generis humani aboleri arbitrabantur, expulsis insuper sapientiae professoribus, atque omni bona arte in exilium acta, ne quid usquam honestum occurreret.

world-situation to come, the mysterious language of images. "The pure doctrine of the lamb -" he announced to them in the best of faith from the unsealed book of the future - "will triumph over the vice-laden polytheism of the all-criminal Babylon. It is true that her power is ruling mightily in the middle of the Mediterranean on her Seven Hills, resplendent with seven heads, her first kings, courted by all the princes of the earth; yet there shine around the throne of the Almighty the influential planets as if they were seven mighty angels, pouring out the cups of wrath over the criminal earth: and from the Euphrates arrive the kings of the Parthians, indeed from all ends of the earth the kings with their armies, like the sand along the sea, in order to wipe out the mighty seductress; from the blood of her horses and armies the earth is flowing already 1600 stadia[14] wide, and indeed already she is fallen! Fallen is she, the all-seductress, and erected on her place is the New Jerusalem of Christendom, out of which now the triumphant teaching of the lamb will rejoice the converted humanity for the course of thousands and thousands of year... etc...etc"

---

[14] *Stadion* or *stadium*, Roman measure of distance; one stadium equals 625 feet or 185 m.

Chapter Eight

Obscured knowledge resulting in erroneous explanation of visual art and imaged tales through the latter Greeks.

None of the ancient peoples still known to us had a sense of artistry as richly and abundantly developed as the Hellenes: all the noteworthy events and changes in the realm of nature, as well as in the individual political states, the individual leaders of the peoples and the heroes were all celebrated through innumerable works of art, temples, public buildings and squares, indeed the dwellings of individual persons were adorned with all kind of visual representations. However differing or even contradictory in details, most of these representations still remained understandable to the community as a whole, as poetic works of different disciplines simultaneously sang and translated the same events. But, with the continual development of separate powers, as the number of the remarkable changes accumulated, prose needed to sever itself from poetry in order to assure their preservation; further, an awakening and expanding science sometimes obscured on purpose the mass of sensual definitions which had

made the old image-language remarkably poly-
signifying, and sometimes attempted to replace it with
de-sensualized form; then it was that the true
comprehension of the old image-tales and visual works
came to extinguish itself, as did later the
comprehension of hieroglyphics, to such an extent that
soon one took names of persons, such as Phaethon,
which designated real objects, indeed heavenly bodies,
as the names of persons and translated them as such
into the new de-sensualized language. On the one
hand, sensual designations, through which abstractions
were suggested, became understood in their gross,
sensual meaning, so that for example the two-bodied
Kekrops was presented to the Athenians as a real
double-bodied creature; on the other hand, beneath the
sensual representations, the transformations and events
themselves, which needed to be understood in their
literal meaning, came to be interpreted as mysteries,
secrets, or aberrations of the senses, conceptions which
had never occurred to their early creators but only to
the late interpreters. Already Philo of Byblos,[15] when

---

[15] Philo of Byblos (Herennios Philon), ca. 64 AD -
141 AD, Greek grammarian, lexicographer and historian,
probably a Roman citizen. Only fragments of his extensive
works are known to us, most of which through quotes by
Eusebius of Caesarea, a Christian author of the 4th century
AD.

speaking about Sanchunjathon,[16] accuses the Greeks of having mixed up their concepts, and foisted recent interpretations upon the ancient myths; in the same way as the more modern, rather unjustly, set out to blame Sanchunjathon " to have declared himself an enemy of any deeper mystical, or, according to his expression, allegorical meaning, and to be a mere zealot for the gross literal meaning of the old god stories, which appear with him to be totally brutish."[17]

---

[16] Sanchunjathon, a Phoenician author, whose extensive works survive only in a paraphrase by Philo of Byblos, itself known only through quotes by Eusebius of Caesarea. According to Porphyry, Sanchunjathon lived before the time of the Trojan wars, close to the time of Moses, "when Semiramis was Queen of the Assyrians." According to the same Porphyry, he wrote the "truest history of the Jews," because he obtained records from Hierolambus, priest of Ieuo. His Creation history has resemblances with Hesiod. Considered for centuries to be a mythical figure, or a fabrication of Philo, Sanchunjathon's writings have been shown to be supported by the XX. century findings of the Ras Shamra tablets of Ugarit, dating back to the 2nd millennium BC, which uncovered extensive libraries of clay tablets in languages and writings forms hitherto unknown, including the first alphabetic writing.

[17] Schelling, Friedrich (1775-1854), *Die Gottheiten von Samothrake.*

Chapter Nine

Erroneous interpretation of the myths by the modern.

During the long lasting battle between the newly arising
Christianity and the old polytheism of the Greeks and
Romans, the first church authors, by name Arnobius,
Augustin, Eusebius, Clement of Alexandria, Lactantius
et al., eagerly endeavored to demolish the ancients
from the ground up, and to load contempt upon all the
knowledge of heathens. Be it on purpose or mistakenly,
they explained such image-tales, which were to be
understood only in a totally indirect, non-intrinsic way -
for instance, the encounter of Mars and Venus - as true
incidents of a human nature, from which the story
becomes ridiculous and unworthy of the divine
character of the gods; or they strained to demonstrate
in these image-tales - in which the images could not
possibly have constituted a coherent unity akin to a
conceptual system of words - apparent contradictions,
for instance, that Apollo appears once as the Sun God,
and then again as the son of the mortal Latona; or to
point out impossibilities, for instance, that gods could
actually die, as, according to the heroes themselves,

many a Jupiter had died, and that even the tomb of one of them was still being shown on Crete. Indeed, the fact that the knowledgeable devotees of the old gods were well able to distinguish between the eternal beings and their visible representations - kings and priests - has been established for a long time; less well known has been the fact that especially the priests of the Chaldeans and Egyptians, offended by the vilification and ridicule heaped on them by the church authors, found themselves prompted to bury in oblivion the treasures of astronomical and medical knowledge which had been preserved in the old script writings, rather than to go on exposing them to their malign detractors.

However strenuously many church authors endeavored to make the allegorical meanings of the so-called polytheists appear laughable, they did not renounce using them for their own purposes, and continued employing them in their exegesis of the biblical stories for many centuries. So, for instance, in Clement of Alexandria,[18] even in the early Old Testament wine already designates the teaching of Christ, and the young ass, bound to the old grapevine,

---

[18] Clement of Alexandria (ca 150 AD - ca 215 AD), Titus Flavius Clement, (Saint), teacher of the Church, probably born in Athens, director of the catechetical school of Alexandria; (*Paidagogos,* I., 5, and II.)

is an allegory for all the peoples who must accept his teaching in the future; according to Rhabanus Maurus[19] jasper, which is found in the Red Sea, represents in a mythical and allegorical sense (he mixes up the two as equivalents, as often happens) the eternal power of faith, conquered through the baptism and suffering of Christ; according to him, the blood colored garnet stands for the glory of the martyrs; chalk for the bond of love with which the believers are cemented together similarly to stones in the house of the spirit... As for the theologians of the 16th century, they famously discovered in any circumstance related in the Old Testament, even in the story of the speaking animal of Bileam, a direct announcement of something similar in the New Testament.

All too much, until recently, the Greek myths have been treated in such a biased way. Until the beginning of the 18th century scholars, who lacked a sense of poetry as well as taste and knowledge, actually endeavored to reduce the bases of all image-tales to mere personal stories, as a consequence of which the masterpieces of the old sensual artists, such as the fall of Phaethon, and the tears of his sisters, hardening into

---

[19] Rhabanus Maurus (ca 780 AD - 856 AD), Benedictine monk, theologian, archbishop of Mainz (Germany). Author of the encyclopaedia: *On the Nature of Things; De Lapidibus,* Book XVII.

amber, must necessarily appear as the elucubrations of some deranged poetic mind; but since the middle of that century, poetic minds - who in their turn are lacking knowledge of history and criticism - alike to the old sophists who denied all reality, even the reality of their own thinking - saw the bases of all myths either as mere affabulations, or as "philosophemes," philosophical propositions clad in poetic dress, so that even Homer's songs about the Trojan war, undeniably rooted in world history, appear to them as a broad allegory about some prince of the house of Cadmeus, leaving us to guess that all older history, in a thousand years from now our Thirty Years War included, will be defined as a fable and an allegory.

Part Two

Change of Orbit of Planet Hesperus and the Ensuing Floods

Chapter One

Displacement of Planet Hesperus.

Among the celestial events of early times there is hardly one that was as momentous as the one which affected planet Hesperus. According to an ancient image-tale of Diodorus,[20] Hesperus was a son or a brother of Atlas, the father of the Hesperides, and a great scholar of astronomy. One day, having climbed Mount Atlas in order to conduct celestial observations, he was carried off by a large storm wind and his body was never found. Because of his piety and his love of humanity, the people brought him divine honors and named the most beautiful star in the western sky after him.

---

[20] Diodorus Siculus, Book III., *60*, Book IV., *27*.

According to Hyginus,[21] Hesperus, as the evening star, was a son of Venus and Cephalus, who on account of his beauty was called by his mother's name, Venus. Yet Diodorus errs evidently in that, because of his insufficient knowledge of hieroglyphics, he does not translate the names of persons, by which celestial and natural features were designated, but instead he explains them in terms of real persons who would have occupied themselves with matters of the heaven or of nature.

That his approach was wrong becomes clearly apparent in the prose telling of said event, as communicated word for word to us by Saint Augustine,[22] quoting the lost work of Varro about the

---

[21] Gaius Julius Hyginus (ca. 64 BC - 17 AD), freedman of Emperor Augustus, superintendent of the Palatine Library, prolific author, most of whose work is los; *Poeticon Astronomicon* (attribution now disputed) Book II., *42*.

[22] Saint Augustine of Hippo (354 AD - 430 AD), Aurelius Augustinus, bishop and doctor of the Church, one of the most important figures in the development of Western Christianity; *The City of God,* Book XXI. ch.8: "Est in M. Varronis libris, quorum inscriptio est de origine gentis Romanae, quod eisdem verbis, quibus ibi legitur, et hic ponam: in caelo, inquit, mirabile extitit portentum, nam in stella Veneris nobilissima, quam Plautus Vesperuginem, Homerus Hesperon appellat, pulcherrimam dicens, Castor scribit, tantum portentum extitisse, ut mutarem colorem, magnitudinem, figuram, cursum, quod factum ita neque antea, neque postea sit. Hoc factum Ogyge rere dicebant

origins of the Roman people:[23] "In the heaven there occurred an extraordinary event; for it happened that the brilliant star, Venus, which Plautus names Vesperugo and Homer 'beautiful Hesperos,' was seen, as described by Castor, undergoing the amazing miracle of changing its color, size, appearance and orbit, such as had not happened ever before, nor since. That this event took place under the reign of King Ogyges was reported by Adrastus of Cyzikus and Dion of Naples, two famous mathematicians. Such an eminent author as Varro would not have considered this to be an extraordinary event if it had not contradicted the laws of nature such as he, albeit incorrectly, understood them; for how could anything run counter to that, which happens by the will of God?" A pious explanation, to which we owe the salvaging of a piece of information about one of the major transformations to have taken place in Nature.

Adrastus Cycenus et Dion Neapolites, mathematici nobiles. Hoc certe Varro, tantus auctor portentum non appellaret, nisi esse contra naturem videretur. Omnia quippe portenta contra naturam dicimus esse, sed non sunt. Quomodo enim est contra naturam, quod Dei sit voluntate?"

[23] Varro, Marcus Terentius, (116 BC - 27 BC), Roman scholar and writer, known as "the most learned of Romans." Author of some 400 pieces, of which only two survive complete, seventy others are known from fragments; *Of the Race of the Roman People.*

The reporters of the event are impressive:
Varro, most learned of the ancient Romans, keeper of
one of Caesar's libraries, and author of several works
among which his history of the Roman people excels
all similar works in sharpness and depth; also the orator
Castor, who according to Guidas originated from either
Rhodes or Galathia and was endowed with the
surname "friend of the Romans." He was the son in
law of the Galatian king and roman senator Dejotarus,
and was executed by the latter, together with his wife,
on charge of having falsely accused him before Cesar.
He was the author or several works on grammar and
history, among which the essays *(Xronika Agnoimata)* as
well as two books about Babylon, one book about the
Nile, and about the rulers of the seas *(Peri
Thalassokrounton)*, all listed by Guidas. Adrastus of
Cyzikus, a proto-historic hero, is mentioned here
probably erroneously in place of Adrastus of
Philippopolis, who was a student of Aristotle and a
commentator of Plato and who wrote several books on
harmony and other subjects.

The prophet Isaiah[24] himself has reported
about the break-up of this star when he called out,
addressing the last toppled king of Babylon: "How hath

---

[24] Isaiah, Biblical prophet, (fl. 740 BC - 701 BC);
Isaiah, Ch.14, *v.12ff*

thou fallen from on high, thou beautiful Morning Star? How hast thou fallen on the Earth, thou who weakened the pagans? Yet thou wast thriving in thy heart: I want to climb high in the sky, and establish my seat above the stars of God; I want to go down onto the Mountain of the Covenant towards the side of Midnight; I want to fly over the high clouds and be alike to the Exalted. Yet to Hell do you go, to the side of the abyss, etc etc..." A newer translator, supposedly closer to the original, renders, in place of "morning star,' "son of red dawn" - but wasn't Hesperus, according to the mythology of the Greeks, a son of Aurora? It is remarkable, furthermore, that Rhabanus Maurus[25] equates the fallen Lucifer to the Dragon in the Apocalypse who, similarly to Typhoeus, was thrown into the abyss after a mighty fight with archangel Michael. Which in turns helps explain why, by means of a tradition of medieval monks, the beautiful Lucifer became confused with and identified as the Devil himself.

---

[25] Rhabanus Maurus, *De Planetis et Stellis*, IX., *16*

Chapter Two

Collision with other heavenly bodies, as the cause of this event.

It would appear that the observations of modern astronomers, according to whom planet Venus, on account of its smallness, would appear to be merely a piece of one formerly larger, which might have been circling in orbit between Mars and Jupiter, and might have been shattered by a collision with a comet, are compatible with these reports.[26] In

---

[26] Note of the Author: Maybe that this change of orbit occurred through the effect of a collision with what was in olden times referred to as a "dragon-star," or comet, about which, according to Rhode (*About The Beginnings Of Our History*, Breslau, 1819) the old Zend Awesta writings of the Farsi give us the following information: : "The Enemy of Nature ran up from the South and found himself in the Zone of Water (i.e. the constellation of the Crab). From there, he flew over the Earth all its length, destroyed everything in the South, and darkness covered everything, as the darkness of night. Boiling hot water rained onto the trees, they died in the wink of an eye. Everything burned down to the root; the earth itself was scorched and barely still existed. It is true that in the heavens the Moon and the Sun

the still available debris of written history, there can be found no report of such a collision, but in the old image-tales, we can find accounts of encounters of Venus with other bodies. For instead, it is said in one that the Sun God betrayed to Vulcan the secret meeting of Mars with Venus and that the betrayed husband imprisoned them both in an adamantine net and offered them to the mockery of Jupiter and of all the assembled gods; according to another, which we

---

followed their course, but the Enemy of Nature fought against the planets, he wanted the destruction of the world: and clouds of smoke flew up from the fires raging in all places. For ninety days and ninety nights the fight took place; then the Enemy of Nature was vanquished and beaten back. At that point Taschter (Jupiter) sent rain and hurled lightning; drops fell, the size of the head of a man, and the water covered the whole earth to the height of a man. Then there came a wind from heaven and in clouds it carried away the water, as if it was the soul in the body; Ormuz then collected the waters in the sea, and he gave them the land to border in. But now the Enemy of Nature broke open the earth from below and since that time he rules over it together with Ormuz, he meddles in everything and brings thousandfold misery, especially in winter..." - Maybe, and even likely so... for we can conclude from several mythological sources that this "dragon-star" did not appear after, but already before the Ogygian flood, for reasons which we will be developing in other places.

will deal with later in greater detail (Part III., ch. 2), it
is told that (planet) Mars constantly pressed Venus,
daughter of Jupiter, with his love; according to a third,
that Venus ravished Phaethon, son of Cephalus (or,
according to others, of Tithonus and Aurora) on
account of his beauty, to make him her priest or temple
guardian on Crete.[27] This latter legend seems either to
stem from a confusion with the Phaethon with whom
we will be dealing explicitly in the third section of this
work, or finds its origins in old Cretan traditions. On
the promontory of Samothrace, which suffered many
changes of shape through fire and waves, Venus,
Pothos and Phaethon were honored in the most
solemn rites, according to Pliny.[28]

---

[27] Hesiod (ca. 700 BC), Greek poet, probably born
in Askra (Boetia), at the foot of mount Helikon, the son of
a destitute immigrant from the coast of Asia Minor. He is
the main source, with Homer, of Greek mythography, as
well as of invaluable information on the daily life in his
times; he seems to have made a living tilling the soil and
tending animals, in surroundings of unremitting poverty,
according to his own words; *Theogony*, and Clement of
Alexandria, *Ad Gentes*.

[28] Pliny the Elder, Gaius Plinius Secundus, (23
AD - 79 AD), Roman author, natural philosopher,
historian; his *Naturalis Historia* in ca 160 volumes is an
encyclopedia of the science of nature in his time; his lost
historical work was a source for Tacitus, Suetonius and
Plutarch. He had an important career in the Roman army
and administration. While prefect of the Roman fleet at

Another similar tale seems to have served Lucian[29] when, in his opuscule, he tells us humorously that once upon a time Endymion, king of the Moon, attempted to send a colony of settlers into the deserts of Lucifer, when Phaethon, King of the inhabitants of the Sun, stepped into his way out of envy, etc.

As the oldest descriptions of heaven are only preserved in images (which we are still using today), the earliest observed changes in the heavens could be handed down to posterity only by means of images and symbols; but an excessively varied amount of meaning remains attached to these, which is a capital drawback for their comprehension.

It must be remarked in addition that planet Venus also carried the name of Letho or Latona with the ancient Greeks, from all appearance harking back to the time when she escaped to Delos. Later, the name of Aphrodite or Venus was reserved to her exclusively, because the double appellation had been up to that

---

Misenum, he died by inhalation of poisoned gas while investigating the eruption of Mount Vesuvius which buried Pompei and Herculanum; *Naturalis Historia,* XXXVI., 4.

[29] Lucian of Samosata (c.120 AD -after 180 AD), Greek rhetorician and satirist, born in Samosata, Eastern Turkey, died in Athens. A brilliant and provocative writer, admirer of Epicurus; *A True Story - Romance,* here referred to by the author, contains a narrative of a trip to the Moon.

time a source of constant confusion between these two
very separate deities.

Chapter Three

The Ogygian Flood and its place in time.

The next consequence of this event was a tremendous flood, which supposedly was named after King Ogyges, of Ogygos of Attica,[30] under whose reign it occurred, and which affected many lands of the Earth, of which several, for example Boetia, Egypt, the island of Calypso and others, received the name of Ogygia, according to Stephanus of Byzantium,[31] while others, like Tyre (in *Dionysios Periegos,* v. 411) carried the additive "Ogygian." According to Nonnus[32], at that

---

[30] Note of the autor: Probably each king had received his name from the old "Ogyg" which is connected to our own [German] *Woge,* "wave," world-encompassing Okeanos, and which according to Bredow means a circle, in Phoenician. As he ruled in farthest protohistory, one designates through the term Ogenisch, Ogenic, everything stemming from the darkest ancient times.

[31] Stephanus of Byzantium (fl. 6th century AD), author of *Ethnica,* a geographical dictionary, largely lost.

[32] Nonnus (lived end of the 4th, or beginning of the 5th century AD), Greek epic poet, born in Panopolis (Egypt). His epic *Dyonisiaca* tells of the expedition of Dyonisus to India and bears resemblance to Indian epics.

time an endless snowfall covered the earth, all the way up on high, so that the highest mountains in Thessaly and the crests of cloud-touching Parnassus were floating in the icy flood.

Moreover, then, according to Solin,[33] a night lasting nine months and longer had covered the earth. Saint Augustine, who has preserved for us the reports about the change of orbit of Venus, adds[34] that authors do not agree about the time of the life of Ogyges. But let us now put together and compare the old authors' inputs, as far as they are still available.

The savant Varro - who divides history into three areas, namely the first from the beginning of mankind to the First Flood, the second from the First Flood to the first Olympic Games (776 BC), and the third from the Olympics to his own days[35] - places in

---

He later converted to Christianity and wrote a poetic version of the *Gospel of John; Dyonisiaca,* III.

[33] Solinus, Gaius Julius (fl. 3rd century AD), Latin grammarian and compiler, author of *De mirabilibus mundi* ("Of the Wonders of the World"); *De mirabilibus mundi,* ch.11.

[34] Saint Augustine of Hippo, *The City of God,* Book XVIII, *3.*

[35] Gaius Julius Censorinus, *De Die natali,* ch.21. "Varro tria discrimina temporum esse tradit: 'primum ab hominum principio ad cataclysmum priorem, quod propter

one of his works[36] the Ogygian flood into the year 1400

---

ignorantiam vocatur adelon, secundum, a cataclysmo priore
ad Olympiadem primam, quod, quia in eo multa fabulosa
referuntur, mythicon nominatur; tertium, a prima
Olympiade ad nos, quod decitur historicon, quia res in eo
gestae veris historiis continentur.' Primum tempus, sine
habuit initium, sine semper fuit, certe quot annorum sit,
non potest comprehendi; secundum non plane quidem
scitur, sed tamen ad mille circiter DC annos esse creditur; a
priore scilicet cataclysmo, quem Ogygium dicunt, ad Inachi
regnum, anni circiter CCCC; hinc ad Olympiadem primam
paullo plus CCCC. Quos solos, quamvis mythici temporis
postremos, tamen, quia a meorium scriptorum proximos,
quidam certum definire volerunt. Et quidem Sosibius
scripsit, esse CCCXCV; Eratosthenes autem, septem et
CCCC; Timaeus CCCCXVII., Aretes DXIV; et praeterea
multi diverse, quorum etiam ipsa dissensio incertum esse
declarat. De tertio autem tempore fuit quidem aliqua inter
autores dissensio, in sex septemve tantummodo annis
versata. Sed hoc, quodcunque caliginis, Varro discussit, et
pro caetera sua sagacitate, nunc diversorum civitatum
conferens tempora, nunc defectus, eorumquem intervalla
retro dinumerans, eruit verum, lucemque ostendit, per
quam numerus certus non annorum modo, sed et dierum
perspici possit. Secundum quam rationem, nisi fallor, nisi
annus, cujus velut index et titutlus quidam est Ulpii et
Pontiani consulatus, ab Olympiade prima millesimus est et
quartus decimus, ex diebus dumtaxat aestivis, quibus agon
Olympicus celebratur, a Roma autem condita DCCCCXCI,
et quidem ex Parilibus unde urbis anni numerantur. - This
passage already appeared suspiscious to the learned
Lindenbrog and others; Scaliger wanted to read instead of
mille et ICC annosonly CICC, which appears unecessary
considering the remarks above.

before the founding of Rome, and has the building of
Thebes as being contemporaneous to the flood ,
placing it into the year 2100 before the augurate of
Augustus (which is the year 717 from the foundation of
Rome); therefore, for the Ogygian flood, he obtains the
date of 2137 years before the birth of Christ; then
placing the Inachian flood, following the opinion of
Gellius[37] and Akusilaos,[38] which are almost exactly
congruent, over 1100 years before Romulus, which
would mean 1854 years before the birth of Christ. In
agreement with this, Solinus declares that after the
midpoint between the Ogygian and Deukalian floods,

---

[36] Varro, *De Re rustica*, Book III., *1*. "Etenim
vetustissimum oppidum, quum fit traditum Graecum
Boeotiae Thebae, quod rex Ogyges aedificaret: in agro
Romano Roma, quam Romulus rex; nam in hoc nunc
denique est, ut dici possit, non quum Ennius scripsit
'Septingenti sunt paullo plus aut minus anni,' (est) Augusto
augurio, postquam inclyta condita Roma; Thebae, quae
ante cataclysmon Ogygi conditae dicuntur, eae tamen
circiter duo millia annorum et centum sunt, etc."

[37] Aulus Gellius (ca 125 AD - after 180 AD), Latin
author and grammarian, his *Noctes Atticae* ("Attic Nights")
contain 20 volumes of notes on all kinds of subjects; *Noctes
Atticae*.

[38] Akusilaos of Argos (ca 5th century BC), only
fragments of his work are known. This particular one is
found in Eusebius, himself quoting Julius Africanus.

six hundred years had passed.[39] Plato who, according to Clement of Alexandria, followed Akusilaos in his own rendition of these events, had put the Ogygian flood into these earlier times, for in the *Critias* he pointedly describes the later Deucalion flood as being the third one.

Some newer commentators, agreeing with Cuvier[40] (*Considerations about the ancient origin of the world* by Dr J. Roeggerath, p. 299) put Varro in contradiction with the indications above, and merely drawing on a suspicious passage from Censorinus,[41] put the Ogygian flood into the year 1600 before the first Olympics, i.e. 2376 BC, failing to consider that this passage does not represent the position of Varro, but the one of Censorinus, and that this author had hurried to add the

---

[39] Solinus, Gaius Julius, *De mirabilibus mundi*, ch. 11.

[40] George, Baron Cuvier (1769-1832), trail-blazing French naturalist and zoologist, one of the founders of paleontology, and author of classical works on comparative anatomy of fossil and living animals. Author i.a. of *Discours sur les révolutions de la surface du globe, Le Règne animal distribué d'après son organisation, Rapport historique sur les progrès des sciences physiques depuis 1789...*

[41] Censorinus Grammaticus, Roman grammarian, fl. 3rd century AD. He wrote about the natural history of man, music, astronomy, philosophy, chronology, mathematics... *De die natali.*

238 years which he himself had lived since Christ to
Varro's year-count; yet others - like the editors of his
fragments - with a reference to the quote above by
Gellius, have Varro fix the date to the year 1854 BC,
without considering that Varro, in the passage in
question, could only have been speaking of the later,
Inachian, flood, not of the Ogygian flood. The
information of Arnobius that "Varro in the first of his
four books about the origins of the Roman people had
proven after careful calculations that from the great
flood to the consulate of Hirtius and Pansa (in the year
38 before JC) 2000 years had not yet come to pass," [42]
also pertains to this latter flood.

The Church authors in general tend to conflate
the Ogygian flood and the Inachian, and even, as does
Hyginus, both of these and the later Deucalionian into
one and the same, apparently for no other reasons than

---

[42] Arnobius of Sica (died ca. 330 AD), Christian
apologist, *Adversus Nationes,* Book V., *8.* "Varro ille
Romanus multiformibus eminens disciplinis, et in vetustatis
indagatione rimator, in librorum quatuor primo, quos de
gente conscriptos Romani populi dereliquit, curiosis
computationibus edocet, ab diluvii tempore, cujus supra
fecimus mentionem, ad usque Hirtii consulatum et Pansae,
annorum esse millia nondum duo." From this passage, the
collectors of Varro fragments concocted the erroneous
proposition: "a diluvio Deucalionis et Pyrrhae *(instead of*
Inachi et Phoronei) ad usque Hirtii consulatum et Pansae,
annorum esse millia nondum duo."

the fact that they did not find in the Hebrew Holy
Scriptures mention of any other floods than the
earliest, the Noachian, and the last one, which occurred
shortly before the Exodus of Moses from the land of
Egypt; the writings of the Aegyptian priests and of
other pagans did not appear to them as divinely
inspired, nor as old as the Mosaic, and therefore were
deemed by them to be false and were to be rejected.[43]
So that Julius Africanus,[44] for instance, referring by
name to Akusilaos, Hellanikus, Philochorus, Castor,
Thallus, Diodorus of Sicily and Alexander Polyhistor,
has this flood occurring at the time of Phoroneus in
Argos, and Ogyges in Attica, and adds moreover that

---

[43] Note of the Author: But let us not forget
that the historic and astronomic chronicles of the
Egyptian priests reach far beyond the age of Moses,
and also contained the major events of the history of
the peoples who then existed; that moreover Moses,
according to the Egyptians, left the country
vanquished, and therefore had to leave behind the
holy books; one must not be surprised that, given the
paucity of the information which he had been able to
carry with him, he ignored most events which did not
directly concern his god.

[44] Julius Sextus Africanus (fl. 3rd century AD),
born in Lybia, he lived in Emmaus and died in Jerusalem
around 250 AD. He wrote *Chronographiai,* a history of the
world in five volumes, from the Creation to the year 221
AD.

Ogyges had lived 1020 years before the first Olympic
Games, therefore 1796 years before the birth of Christ.
He, or one of the other authors whom he cites, must
have misunderstood Akusilaos, for Plato, Varro and
Solinus, who all three had the work of this historian
before their very eyes, did not fail to distinguish
precisely between the two floods.   Unfortunately,
his indications are followed more or less by the other
Church authors. Eusebius, in his *Chronikon*[45], has the
Ogygian flood, as one and the same with the Inachian,
arriving 260 years after Ninus, therefore around 1740

---

[45] Eusebius of Cesarea (ca 275 AD - 339 AD),
bishop of Cesarea in Palestine, referred to as the father of
Church history, a prolific writer whose work has been
largely preserved. He quotes extensively - mostly in order
to refute them - from ancient authors whose work would
otherwise have remained lost to us; *Praeparatio evangelica,*
evang. X., *10: "*-- απο Ωγυγου του παρ εκεινοις αυτοχθονος
πιστευθεντος , εφ ου γενονεν ο μεγας και πρωτος εν τη Αττικη
κατακλυσμος , Φορωνεος Αργειον βασλευοντος , ως
Ακουσιλαος ιστορει , μεχρι πρωτης Ολυμπιαδος , οποθεν
Ελληνες ακριβουντους χρονους ενομισαν , ετι συναγεται χιλια
εικοσιν . ως και τοις προειρημενοις συμφωνει , και τοις εξης
δειχθησεται . ταυτα γαρ Αθιναιων ιστορουντες , Ελλανικος
τοε και Φιλοχορος οι τας Ατθιδας , οι τε τα Συρια Καστωρ
και Θαλλος , και τα παντων Διοδωρος , ο τας Βιβλιοθηκας ,
Αλεξανδρος τε ο Πολυιστωρ , και τινες των καθ ημας
ακριβεστερον εμνηθηραν , και τον Αττικων απαντων ."*

before Christ. According to Syncellus[46] saidflood happened 1235 years before Cyrus (who ruled from 555 BC) and according to Orosius[47] at the time of Ogyges, the builder and king of Eulesis, in Achaea, 1040 years before the founding of Rome, therefore, according to the first in 1790, and to the latter in 1794 before Christ; according to Tatian[48] finally, and to Clement of Alexandria, the flood happens some 400 years before the Trojan war, when, according to him, Inachus, Phoroneus, Aegialeus and Moses are supposed to have been almost contemporaries. It is needless to point out how this mixing up of the events of two from all appearances quite separate periods in

---

[46] Georgius Syncellus (VIII. century AD - died after 810 AD), Byzantine monk and historian. His "Extracts of chronology" *(Ekloge Chronographias),* covered world history from Adam and Eve to the reign of Diocletian;

[47] Paulus Orosius (ca 385 AD - 420 AD), historian and theologian, born in Gallaecia (Northern Portugal). He wrote the *Historiae adversum Paganos* at the suggestion of Saint Augustine, and is the first attempt of a history of the world as guided by God. Despite its dryness and inaccuracy, it was widely translated, including into Arabic, and served as a basis for many later histories.

[48] Tatian (died ca. 185 AD), early Assyrian Christian writer and theologian. His *Oratio ad Graecos* tries to prove the worthlessness of paganism and displays a hatred of all things Greek.

time renders the oldest of these stories most unsecure
and confused.

In Solon already, the priest of Sais reproves the
Greeks for their childish ignorance, for knowing only
about one flood, the one of Deucalion, when several
others had preceded it;[49] indeed Plato expressedly
repeats in *Critias* that during the 9000 years since Sais
had been built, many mighty floods had rolled over the
mountains and plains of Attica, so that the formerly
opulent agricultural land was now reduced to a
skeleton.[50]

---

[49] Plato (427 BC - 347 BC), *Timaeus,*
"...Thereupon one of the priests, who was of a very great
age, said: O Solon, Solon, you Hellenes are never
anything but children, and there is not one old man
among you..."

[50] Plato, *Critias,* "...The consequence is, that in
comparison of what then was, there are remaining only
the bones of the wasted body, as they may be called, as in
the case of small islands, all the richer and softer parts of
the soil having fallen away, and the mere skeleton of
theland being left..."

Chapter Four

Earlier deluges in the time of Noah and Xisuthros.

One of the biggest earlier floods was doubtlessly the one of Noah, which according to the Mosaic, originally Egyptian, documents occurred between the years 2328 and 2385 BC, on the seventeenth day of the second month (ca our November), striking earth with a forty day rain, and a 150 days continuous swelling of the waters, which only subsided on the 27th day of the second month of the following year. The 300 cubits length and 50 cubits breadth of Noah's arch point to the length of the year in those times, the 30 cubit height to the length of the month, and the recurring number seven to the length of the week; the old-Egyptian year by contrast counted already 365 days, since Osiris and Osymandias.[51]

Mount Loubar on Ararat, on which according

---

[51] Name given to an Egyptian Pharaoh by several ancient writers, among them Diodorus Siculus. It is said to refer to Ramses II, of the Nineteenth Dynasty (ca. 1302 BC - ca. 1213 BC).

to Nicholas of Damascus and Epiphanius[52] the arch is
supposed to have stopped, offers to us unexpectedly
the name of the Phrygian-Roman inventor of wine,
Liber Pater.

That Varro himself does not refer to this
particular flood must not faze us, as, given his limited
knowledge of the Egyptian as well as of all oriental
languages, he was only able to use the Greek writings
of his time, who besides the Ogygian did not mention
any other flood.

We are given some information by Abydenus,
a student of Berosus, of a similar flood, if not the very
same one, occurring under Xisuthros, tenth king of
Babylon, who supposedly ruled 440 years before
Ninus.[53] Kronos announced to this king that on the
15th of the month Daesios (February and part of
March) a great flood would destroy the whole of
mankind and enjoined him to save himself and his
family in a boat. The peripheral circumstances resemble
those of Noah. After the waters draw back, he finds
himself on the top of a mountain, enjoins his people to
piety and reminds them to dig up the books which had

---

[52] Epiphanius of Salamis,(ca.310-320 AD - 403
AD), Church father and strong defender of orthodoxy;
Adversus Haereses, Book I.

[53] Eusebius, *Praeparatio evangelica,* Book IX., *12;*

been buried at Zippara, and to live from now on in Babylon. Sip-para, in fact probably Sun-City, from the Indian Sibha, god of the sun, is the later Hierapolis, where, at the occasion of a similar, later flood, we encounter the Scythian Deucalion.

After the Flood, according to Berosus as found in Josephus,[54] humanity had come down from the mountains of Assyria, Media and Parthia (today the lands of Iraq-Adjemi) to settle at first in the plains of Sennar. Already under Babylon's third king Amelon, or Amillarus, the fabulous Danes, which we later get to know as Derceto,[55] had arrived in this land and brought to it the trappings of civilized living.

Whether the flood described in the old Indian writings is the same as the one just mentioned, or if it is even older, we will have to examine elsewhere.

The South Americans as well tell us that once upon a time, at the occasion of a great flood which had descended over all of Peru, they had fled to the mountains and that after it had subsided, they had found the plains inhabited by giants, yet they too were

---

[54] Flavius Josephus (ca.37 AD - 100 AD), Jewish historian who became a protégé of the Roman emperors Vespasian and Titus; *Antiquities of the Jews*, Book I., 4.

[55] Derceto, also known as Atargatis, Syrian goddess whose cult spread to Greece.In Diodorus Siculus, quoting Ctesias, she is the mythical mother of Semiramis.

unable to date this event.[56]

According to Eschwege[57] the Guaykurus of Brasil have a tale of a mighty rain, which in times past had over-flooded the whole earth; according to David Kranz, the people of Groenland tell that the earth had once rolled over, after which event the sea had covered the highest mountains.

A similar legend of the Arabs (transcribed in the "Universal History" of Aini, translated from Arabic into Turk, in vol. 2, and included in *Fundgruben des Orient*, vol. 4, p. 422) reports that Sa, son of Besser and founder of Sais, built a large city in the farthest oasis, surrounded by a fortification wall of 50 ells high and 20 ells broads, and deposited in it all his treasures and his books of wisdom, toi save them from the Deluge. Compare this with the *Reports of Danish Missionaries*, vol. 1, p. 264, were Malabaran priests tell of a past deluge under Vishnu, and a coming destruction of the world under a flood of fire. The Hindustani teachings about the general conflagration of our world system

---

[56] Charles de Brosses (1709-1777), French writer and philosopher; *Histoire des navigations aux terres australes, contenant ce que l'on sait des moeurs et des productions des contrées découvertes jusqu'à ce jour* (1726).

[57] Eschwege, *Journal von Brasilien*, Weimar, 1818, 2, p. 280.

THE SHATTERING OF THE GREAT PLANETS HESPERUS &
PHAETHON

occasioned by a comet can be found in Bedang, also
quoted by Pallas, *Sammlungen historischer Nachrichten über
die mongolischen Völkerschaften,* vol. 2, page 34.

Chapter Five

Fiery eruptions, new islands and loss of Atlantis.

Another consequence of this celestial event were large earthquakes and eruptions which in part had preceded the flood mentioned above. By their effect, the Cycladic islands, among others, were pushed up and, in their middle, according to Aristotle,[58] the celebrated Delos, which received its name either from the eruption of the underground fire or, according to Solinus, because it had become visible only after the flood of Ogyges. The related name Pyrpile, Delos is supposed to have obtained because fire had been invented there, according to Aeglosthenes.[59] When Latona was chased all over the world by the sea serpent Python - i.e. the name of the flood itself - and by the giant Tithon, Neptune, according to legend, lifted up this island from the waves and gave it as a refuge to the

---

[58] quoted in Pliny the Elder, (23-79 AD) *Naturalis Historia,* Book IV., *22.*

[59] *Ibid.*

goddess, who there gave birth to Apollo and Artemis.[60]
Unfortunately, history has not recorded if at the
occasion of these convulsions other islands of the
archipelago of the Cyclades rose from the sea as well -
or if the tearing away of Eubea, Sicily and Britain from
the continent, mentioned in Virgil, Servius and Pliny
among others, occurred then or later. Samothrace at
least was torn off at this time, if not even earlier. The
inhabitant of this island tell us indeed[61] that, even
before the inundations in other lands, the Black Sea
had intruded by the way of the rivers, had broken
through the Kyanaeic Rocks and the mouth of the

---

[60] Note of the Author: The same
description can be found remarkably - if in another
context - in *Revelation* (c.12 v1) "In the heaven, it is
said, there appeared a woman, dressed in the sun,
with the moon at her feet, and a crown of twelve
stars around her head, screaming in the pains of
childbirth; in the same time, a large red dragon with
seven crowned heads and ten horns, who with its tail
slew one third of the stars down onto earth, vomited
a stream of water from its mouth toward the woman,
to drown her and to eat up her child. But the Earth
drank up the stream, and the woman saved herself
into the desert, and her child, a male, was taken in
rapture to god, to lead to the pasture the pagans,
wielding a rod of iron etc, etc, etc..."

[61] Diodorus Siculus (ca.90 - ca.30 BC), *Bibliotheca
historia*, Book V., 47.

Hellespont, and had flooded a great part of the coast of
Samothrace and of Asia.[62]

During an enormous earthquake, a great flood
covered in one day and one night the island of Atlantis
and pushed its remains under the sea. Through the
resulting mud - it had been larger than Asia and Africa
together - the Straights of Hercules remained
unpassable for a long time. That this event should have
occurred at this same time, not earlier or later, is hinted
at, at least in part, by the fact that Plato, in his *Timaeus,*
describes its inhabitants as being so evil as only peoples
of the Iron Age could have been, and in part also by
the fact that there is no reference to it in any of the
later description of the heavens or of natural events.

---

[62] Note of the Author: There are still visible
traces of the fact that the Caspian Sea was connected
to the sea of Azov (according to Pallas, *Voyage Into the
Southern Domains Of The Russian Empire*). The similarity
of the coastlines of Northeastern Siberia with those
of the facing coasts of America at the Bering Straits
clearly suggest that there too, lands were once
connected, and that they could only have been torn
asunder by a mighty natural event.

Chapter Six

The Inachian Flood.

Soon after the Ogygian, another flood occurred, associated with fires running all over earth, which was named after Inachus, the first king of Argos, yet it is confused by most writers with the earlier one. According to the genealogist Akusilaos, quoted by Julius Africanus,[63] who flourished in 600 BC, and who wrote down the history of the kings of Argos basing himself on inscriptions from bronze tablets, Inachus lived 1020 years before the first Olympics, in other words - as these took place in 776 BC - in 1796 BC; according to Syncellus and Orosius, he lived around 1790-1794 BC, according to Varro in 1854 BC and according to Eusebius in 1850 BC. In the image-language of Apollodorus,[64] Inachus is said to be a son of Okeanos and Tethys, or, to put it in common

---

[63] in: *Eusaebii Praeparat. Evang.* Book X., *10.*

[64] Apollodorus, or Pseudo-Apollodorus (born ca 180 BC), author of the three volume *Bibliotheke,* a grand summary of traditional Greek mythology and heroic legends, the only one of its kind to survive from classical antiquity; *Bibliotheke,* Book II., *1.*

language, he had arrived over the sea, coming from
Egypt. From him the Argive river In-achus - i.e. In-
brook, supposedly received its name - unless it was the
reverse... Neptune and Juno having entered into a fight
over the possession of the Argolis, Inachus, as a river
god - or according to others, Phoroneus - dedicated the
land to Juno; in retaliation, Neptune punished the land
with a nine year drought such that he deprived all the
rivers of the country, including the Inachus, of their
waters.[65] According to legend, Inachus ruled for 50
years. His sons and descendants were Phoroneus,
which Arnobius says is an Egyptian,[66] and Aegialeus,
the first king of Argos, second king of Sikyon; Inachus'
daughter was Io, who according to Diodorus
represented Isis, i.e. she was her head-priestess. The
flood occurred at the
time of their kinship.

---

[65] Note of the Author: According to the
grammarian Apion (Clement of Alexandria *Strom.* I.
p230) Moses left Egypt at this time, under the reign
of King Amosis, who is referred to in the Mosaic
writings as Pharaoh. The Jewish leader seems
therefore, in order to enhance the circumstances of
his departure, to take for himself the name of the
king.

[66] Pausanias, *Description of Greece,* Corinth, Book V.,
15.

It had probably started already at the time of
Inachus, or it had been preceded - prepared by - the
nine year drought. At this time, all of Greece, but
especially Attica, according to Diodorus[67], was so
thoroughly devastated that, along with the inhabitants,
all monuments of art and writing were destroyed and
the Egyptians used the opportunity to claim as their
own the earlier inventions of the Greeks in the
domains of astronomy and the sciences.[68] Indeed
according to Julius Africanus the land of Attica had
been so utterly destroyed that it remained without a
king for 189 years, until Kekrops. The Techines, who
were versed in the arts and had a reputation as
magicians especially on account of their knowledge of
meteorology - as Diodorus tells later - had foreseen this
flood and had saved themselves from Rhodes onto the
continent. Of the Rhodians only a few, among them
the sons of Jupiter, had been able to save themselves
onto the mountains of the island. When Helios later

---

[67] Diodorus, *Op. cit.* Book V., *55ff.*

[68] Note of Author: This declaration must
not surprise us, as Diodorus tries at every occasion to
exalt the Greeks at the expense of the Egyptians.
Following Plato, he wants the inhabitants of the
venerable city of Sais in Egypt to be seedlings of the
Athenians.

on, out of love for the island, dried up the waters, he
was honored by the inhabitants as the main deity.

According to the chronicle of Eusebius, this
was also the time when the cities of Sodom and
Gomorrha were destroyed in a rain of fire, and the
surrounding area turned into a swamp of asphalt, the
Dead Sea; in fact, five cities were destroyed at the
borders of Palestine and Arabia, with name Sodom,
Gomorrha, Adama, Seboim and Segor, among which
Sodom, according to Strabo, had a girth of 60 stadia.
Orosius[69] sets this event, which is also mentioned in
Tacitus[70], in the year 1160 before the founding of
Rome, *i.e.* 1914 BC, but he places the Inachian flood,
which he mistakenly calls the Ogygian, in the year 1070
before the founding of Rome, therefore in 1824 BC.

The chronological differences mentioned above
between Varro and Akusilaos can easily be explained
by the fact that one considered the beginning and the
other the end of the fifty year period of the rule of
Inachus as the beginning of the flood, or that Varro
counted too many years for the history of Rome, or by
taking into account Chinese information that the flood

---

[69] Paulus Orosius (c.385-420), *Historiae adversus
paganos.*

[70] Tacitus (ca 56 - ca 117 AD) *Histories,* Book V.,

covered the time of the rule of their three emperors
Phao, Chun and Yu, therefore almost a full century, or,
finally, by supposing that during this period the said
flood, through external effects, renewed itself in several
instances and in different places.

As Phoroneus escaped the flood with his
family, and repopulated the land, one of the authors of
a lost epic, *Phoronis* by name, from which Clement of
Alexandria preserved a few lines for us, names him as
being the first man. On account of the wise laws which
he gave the Argives during his 60 year reign, the latter
author puts him together with Lykurgus and Solon.
Complete information about this flood had been given
by Rhianus in his lost work *Achaica*. As for the poet
Nonnus, he knows nothing about the Inachian flood,
but has the Deucalian flood follow as a second to the
Ogygian, which he considers to be the first.

Chapter Seven

Thessalian or Deucalion Flood - its extension.

After a long period of quiet, there occurred another extraordinary flood, which devastated a great part of Greece, namely Attica, Phokis, Boetia, Epirus and the Peloponese, and on account of its devastations in Thessaly is generally referred to as the Thessalian flood, or after King Deucalion, whose kingdom was particularly affected (according to Varro)[71] it is called the Deucalian Flood. This King ruled in Lykorea on Parnassus. According to the imaged and sensual representations of poets and artists, Deukalion had been able to save himself from perdition on a ship, together with his wife Pyrrha; then, following a divine oracle, he had repopulated the land by throwing stones over his shoulders. (In order to make this mountainous area inhabitable for mankind again, he must necessarily

---

[71] "His tempribus, ut Varro, regnante Atheniensibus Cranao, successore Cecropis, diluvium fuit, quod appellatur Deucalionis, eod quod ipse regnabat in earum terrarum partibus, ubi maxime factum est." Saint Augustine, *City of God.*

have freed the fields and cultures from the stones and
rock and avalanches of debris which must have rolled
down onto them.) According to some, he was a son of
Prometheus, a ruler of the Caucasus, and of Pandora,
or of Klymene; according to others, a son of Haliphron
and of the nymph Jophossa; or of Minos and Pasiphae;
according to others yet, of Isterius and Crete, by which
indications it quickly becomes apparent, as the scholiast
had already pointed out to Apollonius Rhodius,[72] that
several Deucalions must be referred to, who all were
lucky enough to escape the great flood. In today's
Gallic welsh, or Celtic language, Deukal designates a
mountaineer, a Scottish mountaineer, or any
mountaineer; the Scots had, according to their own
legends, moved in coming from the Germanic
Northeast and from Scythia. As there existed
everywhere high mountains, on Crete, on the Istrus
(Thrace?) and on the rocky island of Karpathos, as well
as in our Carpathian mountains and on the Ister, and as
navigation was known at the very least since the time
of Noah, there must have been everywhere cleverly
thinking Deucalions who were able to save themselves
from the general catastrophe by means of boats and by

---

[72] Apollonius Rhodius (ca270 - ?BC; flourished
222 - 181 BC) Hellenistic epic Greek poet, chief librarian
of the Library of Alexandria; *Argonautika,* Book III., *v.1086.*

climbing on heights.

Apollodorus[73] tells us that the whole human race had been destroyed, with the exception of a few, who saved themselves on the highest mountains; Varro too tells (same fragment) "that at the time of the great flood some saved themselves with their possessions into the mountains and on altitudes from which later they easily vanquished those who coming from other mountains attacked them; it so happened that those higher up where called 'gods' and those lower were called 'inhabitants of the earth.'" Of those who had crept up from the plains, it was said in the image-language that they had, instead of feet, snakes. The island of Rhodes and Lesbos were at that time entirely devastated by the deluges and bereft of the majority of their population;[74] the Arcadians are said to have fled to Samothrace. After the flood had eased, the plains of Hellas had become swamps, the air was unbreathable, and agriculture was impossible for a long time; as a consequence of which, war and plague overcame the survivors; the neighboring islands of Kos, Chios, Samos, Rhodes et al., were more easily dried up by the winds, they were repopulated rapidly, and thanks to

---

[73] Apollodorus, *Bibliotheke*. Book I., 7.

[74] Diodorus Siculus, *Bibliotheca historica,* Book V., *55ff* and *81ff.*

their remarkable fertility, they were called "fortunate."[75] (Yet in our time, several of these islands are said to suffer from drought and infertility.)

According to Lucian (writing about the Syrian goddess) the Syrians tell that the Scythian Deucalion[76] had escaped the flood by coming to their land and there had erected, in honor of the great goddess Atargatis, the temple of Hierapolis; according to Pliny[77] the flood had not reached the city of Joppe, built on high rocks by the Phoenicians[78], as a consequence of which the inhabitants endeavored to eternalize the memory of their salvation through the worship of Ceto or Derceto. This heraldic creature - an upright rising woman's head with a dove's wings, the neck of whom ends in a fish body - was also honored among the Celts

---

[75] *Ibid.,* Book V., *82.*

[76] Note of the Author: According to the same Lucian, Deukalion's father Prometheus was enchained in the Scythian Caucasus.

[77] Pliny the Elder, *Naturalis Historia,* Book V., *14.*

[78] Note of the Author: Mela too maintains that this city (today's Jaffa), had been built before the great flood. Earlier it was called Japho, which reminds one of Jophossa, mother of Deukalion.

under the name of Onuava[79] ; as for the Umbrians, a
very powerful Celtic clan inhabiting both sides of the
Apennine, and whose home once extended to the Po
River, they were considered to be the oldest people in
Italy, and were called "Ombrer" by the Greeks because
during the great flood they had been the only ones to
withstand the downpours of rain (ombrous).[80]

All the inhabitants of Phrygia and Lykaonia had
perished in this flood, so that Jupiter entrusted to
Prometheus and Minerva the task to make new figures
of men in clay, and he called upon all the winds to gave
them souls. The place where this occurred was given
the name Ikonium, i.e. the "city of images."[81]

_____

[79] Radloff, Johann Gottlieb, *Keltenthum,* p.400.

[80] Pliny the Elder, *Op. cit.,* Book III., *19.*

[81] Note of the Author: Stephanus gives
additional explanations: "It is said that Ikonium is the
city of Annakos, who is supposed to have lived 300
years; the neighboring peoples having asked the
oracle, how long he would go on living, the oracle
answered that after his death, all would be
annihilated." Hearing this, the Phrygians dissolved
into tears, from which came the proverb: 'crying over
Annakos," meaning, to grieve over all measure. -
According to Guidas, the same Annakos, enlightened
by a divine message, had warned his contemporaries
even before the Deucalion flood, to turn away the
divinely decreed disaster; In some writings this old

The inhabitants of the great Phrygian city of Apamea, which was situated on a high mountain between the rivers Meander and Marsyas, and which carried the nickname of Kibotos or "arch" (i.e. "box"), seem to have escaped the flood. Several of their coins exhibit a box (arch), swimming on the waves, containing a man and a woman. On the box, a bird is sitting, and another bird approaches it, holding a twig in its feet. Close-by, the same human pair is standing with raised right arm on solid ground. On three of these coins, the box has the sign NΩ, while on others only the N is left over.[82] The name No, i.e. Noah, in Phrygian, is not originally the name of a person, but a common name, which represents a "water-man" or a "ship-man," of whom there must have existed many. Moreover, we know from Herodotus that still in the times of Psammetich, the contemporary Phrygians were considered to be one of the oldest people, older even than the Egyptians, from which one is forced to conclude that they were not constituted solely of newly

---

man is also referred to as Kannakos.

[82] Eckhel, Joseph Hilarius (1737-1798), Austrian numismatist, considered the founder of the science of numismatic; *Doctrina numorum veterum,* Tome III., *p.152ff.* This work, in 8 volumes, is still considered an unexcelled reference work.

arrived Dardanians, but that they must have included
ancient autochtonous tribes as well. The flood must
have spread itself over all of Asia Minor, as Asia was
one of the daughter of Okeanos (i.e. "a land risen from
the sea") and the mother of Prometheus and
Epimetheus; according to Diodorus Siculus[83] the flood
had also engulfed Egypt and other lands to the South
despite the fact the Egyptians denied this strongly, as
far as their own country was concerned; we must
dispense with the indications given by other authors,
namely Strabo and Pliny, because it is not always
possible to distinguish if they are to be understood as
effects of the devastations wreaked by the Deucalian
flood, or by an earlier one.

Lacking secure information, we cannot decide
whether the above flood was caused by a new irruption
of the Black Sea into the Mediterranean, or by the
Mediterranean breaking through into the Atlantic
Ocean, or through some other event, to be considered
in the next paragraph. More detailed information had
probably been delivered by the most learned historian
Hellanikus of Lesbos (born 496 BC) in his *Deukaliona*
which is often quoted by Stephanus as *Salmus*.
Hellanikus' work comprised many books, according to

---

[83] *Bibliotheka historica*, Book I., *10*.

Atheneus[84].

In Syncellus, our aquatic hero appears under the name Dukalion, and in Servius both as Deocalio and Deucalion. Lydiatus,[85] in his remarks to the Parian marble-chronicle, calculates this flood to have happened in the year 1553-57 BC, the publisher Humphrid Prideaux, using the chronicle itself, sets it in the year 1529 BC. It must also be remarked that, according to the Parian chronicle, at the beginning of the rule of Deucalion - not unlike the fight of the gods preceding the Inachian flood - a quarrel arose between Mars and Neptune over the latter's son Hallirothius, for which the spot was called Arius Pagus ("Mars-field," or "war-field"). According to Pausanias, Deucalion died in Athens, where he is buried. Like Clement of Alexandria and Nonnus, Servius also admits only two floods, the first under King "Ogiges" of Thebes, the other under Deucalion.

---

[84] Athenaeus of Naucratis (fl.ca 200 AD), *Deipnosophistae*, Book X.

[85] Lydiatus, Thomas (1572 - 1646 AD.), *Disquis. Physiol. de Orig. fontium, & c., Ethnici Philosophi in unius Homeri Poësi omnium artium principiae quaerunt.*

Chapter Eight

Accompanying natural events.

One day, a very heavy fog descended over the Peloponesian cities of Therapna and Dienus, after which the Deucalian flood descended, and then, as Eratosthenes tells us, the cities were swallowed, first by an earthquake, then by the sea.[86] This tremendous earthquake also had laid waste the already considerable city of Athens, with its mighty fortifications reaching all the way to the Eridanus and Ilissus, and including the mountains Pnyx and Lykabetus. The irrupting flood carried down the debris to the sea.[87] According to Apollodorus[88] Jupiter sent great deluges from heaven in order to obliterate the human race of the bronze age;

---

[86] Note of the Author: See Tzetses about the *Kassandra* of Lykophoron (n. 591), and Rote about Steph. Byz. at Bura. Heyne opinionates quite wrongly in his comment on Apollodorius that nobody in the Peloponese knew about this flood.

[87] Plato, *Critias.*

[88] Apollorus, *Op. cit.*, Book I., 7, 1, 2.

and according to Nonnus[89], mighty snowfalls covered
the whole earth. According to Aristotle, a huge winter
descended over all of nature, but especially over
ancient Greece.[90] As reported by other Greek authors,
(Lucian, *De Dea Syra*), the earth opened wide and all of
a sudden great amounts of water poured out; the rivers
swelled to mighty streams and the sea came in close
until all the waters were united in a single flood, and
the whole race of humans was eradicated. For nine
days and nine nights, the Thessalian Deucalion sailed
over the open sea, until finally his ship landed on
Mount Parnassus. (According to the Parian Marble-
Chronicle, he fled from Lykorea before the flood to
join Kranaus, in Athens, where he dedicated a temple
and sacrificed to Jupiter, his savior.)

Poseidon, the ruler of the sea, the earth-shaker,
tore open a breach through the mountains, through

---

[89] Nonnus, *Dyonisiaca*, Book III.

[90] Note of the Author: Aristotle, *Meteorol.* I
c.14. :"For as the seasons are followed by winter,
after a great movement of the celestial bodies there
also follows a very great winter and a mighty deluge;
yet the deluge does not originate in one and the same
place, but does as the one we call Deucalionian Flood
in the land of Greece; and another one of Old
Greece, around Dodona, where the Achelous
changed its bed in many places..."

which the Peneus river then flew without obstacle to
the sea[91] and Thessaly turned into an expanse of lovely
meadows. In Athens, the flood lost itself into a hollow
in the Temple of Zeus through which now wheat flour
and honey were poured in a sacrificial offering; similar
rites were accomplished in Hierapolis, in Syria, where
the Scythian Deucalion dedicated a temple to Atargatis.
Still in Lucian's times, people from all over Syria, as
well as from Arabia and from beyond the Euphrates,
gathered there twice a year and, in memory of the
disaster which had been visited upon them in the time
of Deucalion, they poured sea water into the cavity,
and climbed on trees and on high mountains.

According to L. Ampelius and to Hyginus,
Deucalion, on account of his piety, was finally
emplaced into the Heavens, where he now shines as
the constellation of the water-bearer, Aquarius;
according to Herodotus,[92] Pausanias[93] and Antiochus
quoted in Clement of Alexandria, the Athenians had
first named this constellation after their king Kekrops,

---

[91] Herodotus (484 BC - ca 425 BC), *The Histories,*
Book VII., *129.*

[92] Herodotus, *Op. cit.* Book III., *53.*

[93] Pausanias (2nd century AD), probably born in
Lydia, Greek geographer and traveller; *Description of Greece,*
Book I., *18, 27.*

at the end of whose 50 year rule the catastrophe had occurred.

Chapter Nine

Setting the date of the flood.

The date of this mighty event falls, according to
Varro,[94] in the nine-year reign of Kranaus, successor of
Kekrops in Attica, a date with which Syncellus is in
agreement.[95] In addition, he connects the event with
the burning up of Phaethon over Ethiopia, but he sets
the time as the year of the world 3995, or 14,659 BC.
(He has Danaus arriving in Greece around 1410 BC,
only). Eusebius puts both events 229 years after the
Ogygian Flood, and even before the Phenician
Hercules Deuso, and before the exodus of Moses from
Egypt, into the year 490 after Ninus, which according
to his method of calculation would be equivalent to the
year 1511 BC, and would correspond to the year 1537
of Solinus, who has 600 years passing between the
flood of Ogyges and the last one. It is therefore quite
unecessary to change the DC years into CC, as does

---

[94] In: Saint Augustine of Hippo, *The City of God.*

[95] Syncellus, *Ekloge Chronographias.*

Salmasius.[96] (This Hercules is probably identical with
the Idaean Hercules, whose descendant Klymenus, 50
years after the flood of Deucalion, reinstated the
Olympic games, first founded by Hercules himself.
According to the Parian Marble Chronicle, probably
the most trustworthy document about these events,
Deucalion acceded to the kingship at Lykorea in the
ninth year of the rule of Kekrops (who, still according
to the same document, began his reign in 1582 BC) - in
1574 BC, therefore; in the fourth year of Kranaus',
Kekrops' successor's rule, in 1529 BC, he fled, forced
by the arrival of the flood, first to Athens; in the year
1523 BC, after the death of Deucalion, he additionally
took dominion over Thermopylae, and created the
Amphyctionic League.[97] This information of the Parian
chronicle is at variance by 20 and a few years from the
chronology of Eusebius.

Orosius, on the other hand, places this flood
together with the Ethiopian plague into the reign of
Amphictyon, the second ruler after Kekrops, into the

---

[96] Claudius Salmasius or Claude Saumaise (1588 -
1653), French classical scholar.

[97] The Amphyctionic League was a Greek
religious organization created more accurately in 1100 BC
to administer the temples of Apollo in Delphi and of
Demeter near Thermopylae. It claimed to have been
created by Deucalion.

year 810 before the founding of Rome; but he puts the
fall of Phaethon, as well as the ten plagues of Egypt,
preceding the exodus of Moses, into the year 805
before the founding of Rome, therefore the prior event
into the year 1564 BC, and the latter
into 1559 BC. Diodorus[98] has this flood pouring down
over Rhodes and Lesbos not too long before the arrival
of Danaus and Cadmus, in fact seven generations (233
years) after the life of argivian Xanthus, the brother of
Inachus. If he was aligning himself with Akusilaos, his
indication would point at the year 1563-64 BC,
consequently fitting with the indications of Orosius;
but again, in another place,[99] he seems to consider the
Inachian and the Deucalion floods, if not as one and
the same, then still as very close in time.

Clement of Alexandria places the exodus of
Moses into the lifetime of Inachus, in fact, into the year
1646 BC - but the flood of Deucalion, which he calls
the second flood, and the fire of Phaethon, he places
four generations later (of which three, according to
him, represent a century), into the time of Krotopus,
ruler in the Peloponnese, which gives us, according to
his most distant calculation, 1514 BC. He only bestows

---

[98] Diodorus Siculus, *Bibliotheka historica*, Book V.,
55ff and *81ff.*

[99] *Ibid.* Book V , *60-61.*

onto Moses a higher age in order to claim for his godly hero a greater respect among the pagans.

As this terrible flood had devastated a great part of the inhabited earth, and as yet more floods and terrifying events had followed on its heels, we must not be surprised to find that the descendants of the overwhelmed survivors could only dimly remember these events, and even got to confuse them with others, that were similar.

We would be able to decide upon the date of this event much more precisely if the great Aristotle had communicated to us the calculations he made on the subject, or if experience had been able to verify his (and others') astronomical claim, namely that after every "Great Year" of 19 years - or even more so, after each great World Year - a succession of deluges and fires occurs.

Moreover, when Clement and Nonnus designate the Deucalian flood as the "second" one, we must not let ourselves be induced in error, for authors with an earlier knowledge of proto-history, such as Plato (in *Critias*) and Varro emphatically call it the third one (Deucalion). The celebrated Rhabanus Maurus, who still held before his eyes many now lost works of

the ancients, names[100] the Noachian as the first, the
Ogygian at the time of Jacob as the second, and the
Deucalian, at the times of Moses and Amphictyon, as
the third.

---

[100] Rhabanus Maurus, *Encyclopedia, On the Nature of
Things,* Book IX., *21,* De Diluviis.

Part Three

The shattering of planet Hesperus

Chapter One

Phaethon, at first a planet between Mars and Jupiter.

Already in centuries past, astronomers have pointed out that in the empty space between Jupiter and Mars, some large planet should be orbiting the sun, and the moderns have indeed discovered there four smaller planets, by name Ceres, Pallas, Juno and Vesta, which they have explained as being the partial debris of a large planet which had been shattered there. The ancient Greek image-tale myths, which were recorded even before the invention of the alphabet, suggest the existence of a planet which, because of its brilliance, had received the earlier name of the sun, Phaethon, i.e.

the bright one[101] but which through collision with another body had been shattered. "O Solon, Solon," exclaims the wise priest of Sais in Plato's *Timaeus* "-you Greeks are still only children, and there is not one old man among you; for you are newborns of the mind and possess not even an original clue about the traditions of the ancient past, not an ounce of wizzened wisdom. The reasons of this are the many and varied annihilations which have hit mankind and will continue to be visited upon it. The greatest of those happened through outbreaks of fire and through floods; the other, lesser ones, through numberless other accidents. For your own tale of Phaethon who, being the son of Helios, once climbed on his father's chariot and who, unable to keep to the father's path, set afire the whole surface of earth and who, hit by lightning, was shattered to pieces is, however much it may look like a fable, quite true. For there occur changes in the orbit *(parallaxis)* of the heavenly bodies which circle the earth and heaven, as a consequence of which, at long intervals, there occur devastations on the earth through

---

[101] Nonnus, *Dyonisiaca,* Book XXXVIII.
                                    -- Sol vero
Filio dedit habere suum nomen testi formae
Conveniens, divini enim semper fulgurante fronte
Solis patris currebat cognatus splendor.

immense fires;[102] then those who live in mountains or on high, dry places are exterminated in much greater numbers than those who live by rivers and on the seashores. But the Nile, who is in all things so benevolent to us, wards away from us such misfortunes..."

These devastations of the earth and

---

[102] Note of the author: Similar conceptions of Aristotle and other Greeks we find in Censorinus *(De Die Natali, c.18)*. "Est praetera annus, quem Aristoteles maximum potius, quam magnum, appellat; quem solis, lunae, vagarumque quinque stellarum orbes consiciunt, quum ad idem signum, ubi quondam simul fuerunt, una referuntur (revertuntur) cujus anni hyems summa est *kataclysmos,* quam nostri diluvionem vocant; aestas autem *expyronis,* quod est mundi incendium. Nam his alternis temporibus mundus tum exignescere, tum exaquescere videtur. Hunc Aristarchus putavit esse annorum vertentium duum millium CCCCLXXXIV., Aretes Dyrrhachinus quinque millium DLII., Heraclitus et Linus decem millium CC∞, Dion XMCC ∞ XXCIV., Orpheus C MXX., Cassandrus tricies fexies centum millium; alli vero infinitum esse, nec unquam in se reverti existimarunt. Sed horum omnium *pentaetiridas* maxime notandis temporibus Graeci observant, id est, quaternum annorum circuitus, quas vocant Olympiadas, etc." - Yet more calculations can be found in Achilles Tatius Isagoge's *Phaenomena,* quoted in Petavius' *Doctrina temporum.*

annihilations of mankind appear to Plato like as many renewals and rejuvenations. In his descriptions of such destructions through fire and flood, the philosopher follows, according to Clement of Alexandria,[103] the historian Akusilaos. Aristotle relates similar things[104] and so does, after him, Apuleius:[105] "Often have we heard that through great earthquakes the earth opened itself, and swallowed cities and peoples; we have heard that through breaking clouds whole lands were washed away; that even portions of continent were turned into islands by waters rushing on from elsewhere, and that other islands could be reached by foot all of a sudden, the sea having receded. What? Who does not remember that through winds and storms cities have been leveled? What? When raging fires came down from clouds, when the lands of the East were set afire, as some believe, by the fall of Phaethon, and the lands of the west suffered equal devastation through deluges and inundations? (...)" The rain of fire which, around the year 1914 BC annihilated the five cities in Asia has already been mentioned in Part 2.

---

[103] Clement of Alexandria, *Stromata*, Book I.

[104] Aristotle, *On the Cosmos*, c.

[105] Apuleius, (ca 125 AD - after 170 AD), born in Numidia (i.e. Algeria), Roman poet and novelist, generally of a humorous and bawdy vein; *De mundo*,

Chapter Two

Traces of residual knowledge in the names of the neighboring planets.

The image-tale of the end of Phaethon had long since become a fable no longer understood in its true meaning, when the name of Phaethon still lingered on as the name of a planet that had disappeared in earlier times. Witness, for instance, Aristotle[106] and Apuleus[107] where the planets are listed in the following succession, and under the following names:

1. Phaenon (the scintillating) or Saturn (Nemesis for the Egyptians);
2. Phaethon, also Jupiter (Osiris for the Egyptians);
3. Pyroeis (Fire-star) or Hercules (for the Egyptians), also Ares or Mars;
4) Stilbon (the radiant one), for some Hermes or Mercury, also (for the Egyptians), Apollo;
5. Phosphorus or Lucifer, for some: Venus, for others:

---

[106] Aristotle, *Mirabilibus Auscultationibus* or *On Things heard*, c.1.

[107] Apuleus, *Op. cit.*

Juno or Junonia;

6. Helios or Sol (for the Egyptians, the fourth planet);

7. Selene or Luna;

Yet in Hyginus,[108] more in accordance with the old fables, the list is the following:

1. Jupiter or Phaethon (in Eratosthenes, Phaenon). According to Heraklides Pontikus Prometheus, when he fashioned men, had made Phaethon so beautiful that Jupiter, inflamed with desire, sent Mercury to call him to himself and make him immortal. This is how he was lifted up among the stars.

2. Sol, for others, Saturn; as Eratosthenes says, this planet acquired the name Phaethon after the son of Sol who, hurled by Jupiter into the river Eridanus, had been placed into heaven by his father.

3. Mars (named Hercules by some) who follows the Venus star - according to Eratosthenes for the following reason: when Vulcan had espoused Venus, his precautions prevented Mars to find access to her any longer, so that Mars could achieve nothing more than having his star appear to follow the star of Venus. But when Amor inflamed him violently, Hyginus designated his state by calling the star Pyroeis.

4. Venus, under the name of Lucifer, which some call

---

[108] Hyginus, *Poeticon Atronomicon*, II., c.42.

Juno. In many stories it is told that the star is called
Hesperus. It appears to be the largest of all. Some
maintain that Hesperus is a son of Aurora and
Cephalus and more beautiful than any other, for which
reason he entered into competition with Venus for
preference; Eratosthenes even says that Hesperus
himself is called Venus for this reason, and that he
appears by sunrise and sunset, and therefore carries the
names of Lucifer and Hesperus.

5. Mercury, also under the name of Stilbon; he is small
and bright and is supposed to be dedicated to the god
Mercury because this god was the first to order the
succession of the months and to have studied the paths
of the stars. Euhemerus[109] maintains that Venus, at
first, had ordered the constellations and had explained
them to Mercury.

According to Hyginus' list the name of
Phaethon, long after the fall of its bearer, was still
assigned to his two neighboring stars; just as later on in
Hyginus, Hesperus was a son of Cephalus and Aurora,
the first Phaethon, whom Venus followed with her

---

[109] Euhemerus (fl. around 316 BC), Greek
mythographer, known for a rationalizing method of
interpretation which treats mythological accounts as
reflections of actual historical events.

love,[110] was a son of these two. Under the name of Mercury, who is supposed to have ordered the months, we must here understand the Egyptian Thoth.[111]

---

[110] Hyginus, *Poetikon astronomikon*, II., c.2.

[111] Note of the author: this changing designation is found in older authors concerning the names and signs of metals, insofar as these are considered to be outpourings of the heavenly bodies. So for instance Zeus is sometimes iron, Mars the metal electrum, mercury tin; sometimes Saturn, sometimes Venus, are gold; sometimes the sign for electrum resembles the sign of the constellation of the crab, which otherwise represents iron; also Phaethon, otherwise a by-name of Jupiter, represents electrum. More about it in Jo. Matth. Gesneri "Praelectio de Electro Veterum" in *Commentt. Soc. Gotting.* T. III. p.74-79.

Chapter Three

Ovid's image-tale of Phaethon

Once it had degraded to a fable, the later poets handled
the image-tale of Phaethon each in his own way, related
it to this event or that, and embellished it in varying
ways. Several of their descriptions, like the eponymous
tragedy of Euripides, are unfortunately lost. Ovid, in
his *Metamorphoses*, almost entirely imitated from the
Greeks, depicts the event in the following way,
apparently basing himself on Hesiod:[112] After Jupiter
had transformed Lykaeon, who had maliciously offered
him human flesh to eat, into a wolf in punishment, and
had destroyed his house in a fire, he decided together
with the assembled gods, to annihilate the vicious
human race through a flood. Only Deucalion and
Pyrrha escaped this flood and repopulated the earth
anew, after having brought sacrifices to Jupiter. After
a masterly description of this event, the poet delivers
some transition images, to begin with, the creation of
Python (the sea serpent), i.e. the stagnant waters, by

---

[112] See the fragment from a lost work of his
quoted by Hyginus, *Fabulae*, 154. In his still available
Theogony, Hesiod mentions only the other Phaethon, son of
Aurora and Cephalus.

Phoebus; then the metamorphosis of Daphne, daughter of Peneus, into an olive tree, the branches and leaves of which now crown the heads of the winners of the Pythic games; then the story of Io, daughter of Inachus, which Jupiter, in order to save her from the jealousy of Juno, transforms into a cow. Her son was Epaphus, whose tempels are connected with those of Jupiter. Equal to Epaphus in spirit and years was Phaethon, sired by Sol. When, filled with pride one day Phaethon boasts about his divine origins, Epaphus mocks him as a simpleton who, filled with vanity, will believe anything that his mother tells him. Phaethon wails about the insult and, on the counsel of Klymene, runs to Sol, begging him for authorization to lead the chariot of the sun for one day. Things went well to begin with; but the horses soon felt the unexperienced hand of the charioteer, they left the habitual path and lifted themselves up first to the stars of the cold North, than dove too deeply into the direction of earth. The Triones and Bootes tried in vain to flee from the fire into the cool waters of the sea, and the otherwise cold-stiffened Dragon swelled up in new anger. Seized with dizziness when looking down from the great heights, and shaking with fear at the larger half of the way still to be covered, the weak charioteer sees the threatening constellation of Scorpio and lets the reins fall out of his hands in terror. Wildly now the horses go back and forth in the heaven and put the sky and earth aflame.

All food-giving plants burn up, all wells, springs and seas dry up; great, compact cities are turned into ashes together with their inhabitants, whole peoples are destroyed; mountains and forest flare up in fires; Athos is burning, as are the Taurus of Cilicia, Imolus and Deta; Ida, famous for its springs, is dry, also the Helikon, holy to the muses, and the as yet uncelebrated Hemus. With two separate sources of fire Etna is burning to immeasurable heights, the double summits of Parnassus are burning, the Eryx, the Cynthus and Othrys, the finally snow-freed Rhodopus, the Dimas, Dindyma and Mykale, and the holy Kithaeron. To no avail is the frost to the land of the Scythians; the Caucasus is ablaze, also Ossa and Pindus and, higher than both, Olympus; also the airy Alps and the cloud-high Apennine. Phaethon sees the whole earth in flames, breathes in hot air as if coming from a glowing furnace, and feels under him the chariot turning red hot. Enveloped in ashes and smoke clouds, he does not know where to go and lets himself be carried away by the horses, unconscious. That is when the people of Aethiopia are supposed to have turned black, as their blood was drawn to the surface of their bodies;[113] then

---

[113] Note of the Author: About the influence of the air, the sun and the particular lifestyle on human skin coloring, one may consult the *Remarks*

did Lybia turn into a desert of sand, as the heat bereaved it of all waters. The wide-bedded rivers no longer flow securely: the Tanais goes up in vapor clouds, also the old Peneus, and the Phokaian Erymanthus; the Xanthus also went up in vapor, as did the yellow Lykormus and the serpent-like Meander, the Melas of Mygdonia [Phrygia] and the Eurotas of Taenarum. The Euphrates in Babylone burned, the Orontes, and the rapid Thermodon, the Ganges, the Phasis and the Ister. Boiling with heat are Alpheus and Sperchius; the gold of the Tago flows in streams of fire, and singing swans are boiled in the middle of the Kaystrus; the Nile's mouths become seven dusty dry valleys. The same fate dries up the Hebrus and Strymon and the rivers of the Hesperides: the Rhenus, the Rhodanus, the Padus, the Tiber; the whole earth bursts and through the clefts, daylight finds its way to Tartarus and frightens the king of the Netherworld. The sea shrinks and what was until then an expense of water, is now a field of dry sand; mountains arise, which before had been covered by the sea, and the scattered Cyclades are multiplied. The fire is threatening the poles of heaven, and Atlas barely manages to carry the glowing sphere when, touched by the supplications of Earth, Jupiter with his lightning

---

about a journey around the World, by Reinh. Forster, Berlin, 1783.

bolt separates the charioteer from his chariot and through enormous opposite fires stops the general conflagration. With burning hair, seeming like a falling star, Phaethon is precipitated from on high, through the air, and is received, far away from his home, by te waves of the great Eridanos. The Hesperidic Naiades bring the smoking corpse to a hill and set on it a stone memorial. His father covered his face in mourning, one whole day passed without the appearance of the sun, and the world was lit only by the fires. Klymene ran about the earth like one insane, mindlessly, and threw herself onto the marble tomb of her son. For four moons his sisters, the Heliades of the Eridanos, wept over him, until they took root as poplar trees, whose constantly running tears are changed in the river into amber. Kygnus, Phaethon's relative and friend, powerful ruler of the Ligurians, left his kingdom, came to the Eridanus and turned into a lamenting swan. Phoebus then refused to take up again the reins of the sun chariot but finally, moved by the prayers of all the gods and the threats of Zeus, resumes driving the chariot again. The King of the gods tried to repair the evil done on earth.

Chapter Four

Explanatory remarks

Granted that our poet added here and there many ornaments to the beautiful old image-tales, which of course he no longer quite understood - a historical truth still shines through the whole of his source material, in part thanks to the internal, logical coherence of the tale, in part through the fact that this material coincides with the traditions of other peoples. The obscuring of the sun lasting one full day coincides, according to the calculations of some, with the Egyptian eclipse which according to the Moses tradition occurred shortly before the exodus of the Jews out of Egypt. Epaphus, who according to Hyginus[114] was a son of Jupiter and of Io, herself a daughter of Inachus, was the builder of Memphis and the ruler of Egypt; according to Herodotus, he was worshiped there as Apis. Literally translated, the name designates an enemy, an adversary, and in the case in point, possibly a satellite of Jupiter[115] who, edged by a

---

[114] Hyginus, *Fabulae.*

[115] Note of the author: In the holy bulls Mnevis and Onuphis, as well as the holy cow of Momemphis, the Egyptians seem to have represented

comet which we will refer to later on, entered into a hostile collision with Phaethon. The latter evaded towards the North, as suggested by the succession of the constellations mentioned, and exploded on its wild, erroneous course sometime in October, when the sun enters the constellation of Scorpio. The greatest amount of debris fell into the Baltic[116] and the Eridanus, which is the amber river of the Teutonic North, about which we will speak in detail later. Its break up now furnishes us with an explanation for the great desert expanses of sand in the North of our country, which stretch over formerly fertile lands, as well as for the many mountain ridges, thrown up this way and that, which are found in the Alps and other mountains, and which often show no relationship with what lies underneath them. In areas where the burning

---

the three other secondary planets.

[116] Note of the author: According to Aristotle, (*On Things heard*, c.82) Phaethon fell into a sea, not far from the (Italic) Eridanus, which he still considers to be the original amber river. On the amber islands at the delta of this river, which had been corresponding with the amber trade from the Baltic to the Adriatic, one could still see in his own time two extremely old figurative columns of Dedalus and his son Icarus, one made of tin, the other of brass, fashioned when Daedalos fled from Minos.

debris fell in great number, even the rivers must have vaporized, or they changed their course, or disappeared into the clefts of the earth when those burst open. Our Rhine, which at this occasion is mentioned in myth for the first time, and which had formerly consisted merely of a chain of large lake-valleys, seems to have become a flowing river only then, through the breaking open of the obstructing barriers containing it in its valley.

Chapter Five

Continuation. Wanderings of the Ligurians towards the North.

It is remarkable that Kygnus, the ruler of the mighty Ligurians, whose constellation is ever since shining in the Northern sky, should come to Phaethon on the Eridanus in order to bewail his friend in the guise of a swan and that in the same time, in Hecataeus of Abdera[117] swans appear as the friends of the Hyperboreans: "Apollo's priests are the sons of Boreas and Chion, three brothers in number, six cubits in height. When these celebrate the feast of Apollo at the fixed time, there fly up, from the so-called Ripaic mountains in their lands, endless clouds of swans which hasten towards the temple and, after having circled over it, and in so doing having consecrated it, land in its large, admirable precinct. As soon as singers and string players elevate their harmonic song to the

---

[117] Hecataeus of Abdera (ca 550 BC - ca 476 BC) Greek historian and sceptic philosopher, who wrote on Egypt *(Aegyptiaca)* and *On the Hyperborean;* quoted in Claudius Aelianus (ca. 175 - ca 235 AD) *De Natura animalium,* XI., c.1.

god, the swans join in; not wildly and cacophonously but, as if guided by the choirmaster, in a competitive zeal continuing the festive song, and sustaining with their harmonies the most expert singers. After the completion of the festive song, the winged chorus leaves, having fulfilled its customary obligation towards the godhead, having participated in the glorification of the god for one full day, having joined in the song and rejoiced the audience." The spring migrations of endless numbers of waterfowls to the North are well known; in Apollo's sanctuary, which was already honored by the Celts, it was forbidden to hurt them; one might well have been able to predict the approach of their flocks by several days by observing the arrival of their scouts, and fix the day of the feast accordingly.

A historic trace of the migration of the Ligurians into our North, after it had been devastated by the aforesaid natural catastrophe and emptied of its people, can still be found in the names of the Ligurians, whose many tribes were still present to the east of the river Elbe in the times of Tacitus and Ptolemy. It is true also that in later times, Ligurians (they were called by that name by the Romans), according to the reports of Scylax[118] and others, migrated out of Iberia into the

---

[118] Scylax of Caryanda (VI. century BC). In 515 BC, he explored the course of the Indus River. *The Periplus of Pseudo-Scylax* is a compilation written in the III. century

regions of the Mediterranean and the Po; still, weren't Celts installed almost everywhere along the whole southern coast of Iberia, as shown in the Kelthentum,[119] and among them the Belgi, Titthi and Germans?

The poets additionally report that the inhabitants of the banks of Eridanus wear black clothes in sign of mourning since the fall of Phaethon; probably merely a beautified reference to the fact that, already then, the Henetians and Venetians, being miners and collectors of amber, wore miners' overalls. It may be true that the Ethiopians' complexion darkened because, as the axis of the earth shifted during this event, the hot latitudes now settled over their heads.

AD.

[119] Radloff, Johann Gottlieb, *Kelthentum*, p. 282.

Chapter Six

Image tales of this and other heavenly occurrences in Nonnus.

Similar informations about this and other heavenly events are given us by the Greek-Egyptian Nonnus[120] in his heroic poem on Dionysos:

1. About the flood of Deucalion, he tells us[121] that Jupiter had devastated the whole earth with fire because the Titans had killed and torn to pieces his and Proserpina's son Zagreus, he being the first Dionysos (Osiris); in order to staunch the general conflagration, he then called up the rain floods from the North Pole, and raised the seas up to the summits of the mountains. Only Deucalion saved himself by means of a boat in

---

[120] Note of the Author: This poet, who was born in Panopolis in Egypt and was still alive at the beginning of the 5th century, had studied in Alexandria and had finished the above work before he converted to Christianity. Regarding India, Stephanos of Byzantium often refers to his writings, considering them to be historical and geographical truths.

[121] Nonnus, *Dyonisiaca*, VI.

Thessaly and repeopled the earth. The excellent
rendition of this tale is deserving particular attention,
but as it does not contribute any new insight into the
dating of the event, we must for the time being leave it
aside.

2. More significant for us are his indications about
Phaethon's wreckage. Hermes (Mercury) prophesizes
indeed[122] to Dionysos that, after his victory over the
Indian, still in the offing: "Then willst thou, having
chased far away this thick impenetrable darkness, shine
next to Ares (Mars) in the heavens, to the Sun God
alike; a miracle, never heard of during the course of the
ages, since Phaethon was toppled down half-burned
from the carriage of the sun into the river Keltos[123] and
the Heliades as quaking poplars on the hills of the
Eridanos bewail the bold youth with sighing leaves. [124]
Dionysos was forthwith filled with hope of victory, and
wished to hear more about this event which had
brought such misfortune upon the Celts of the West
and about the transformation of the Heliades into

---

[122] *Ibid.* XXXVIII.

[123] Ποταμω δε εκρυπτετο Κελτω ."

[124] Και θρασιν ηβητηρα παρ οφρυσιν Ηριδανοιο /
Ηλιαδες κινυρισιν ετι στεναχουσι πετηλοις ."

poplar trees, whose shiny tears dropped from the quacking leaves into the river."

The ever-articulate Mercury follows then with the tale of the marriage of Okeanos with Tethys, and the birth of Klymene, in whom Helios became inflamed. Then he describes "the joy of old Okeanos, who rocked the little Phaethon in his hands - yet in evil portent let him fall into the water; there follow the many child-plays of Phaethon, for instance how as a still beardless youth, in the gardens of his sister Lampetia, in Thrinakria (Sicily), imitating his divine father, he attached four lambs to his little chariot and goaded them on with a lash of flowers. Fortified through these exercises, having grown into a young man, he once asked his father, sitting in his lap, for the permission to drive the heavenly chariot. The father turns down the request on understandable grounds, but gives in when the boy starts crying and his mother joins in in teary supplication. He hurries to climb onto the carriage and his father hastens to teach him about the twelve constellations of the zodiac, about the paths of the planets, of Jupiter, of Mars etc, leaves him with this viatic, and off he goes. His loving mother jumps with joy, but the father is seized with fear. On the top of heaven then the youth watches in amazement the numberless shapes and stars, and in the center of the cosmos, he sees the earth fixed still, with her numberless people, high rocks, rivers and with the

winding Okeanos; meanwhile, the horses, held fast no
longer, leave their customary path. The use of the
fiery lash, against which Lucifer warns him in vain,
drives the horses ever wilder, and makes them go too
far south, then again too far north, storming in the
direction of Orion and Bootes. From the turbulence
seizing the aether, the axis of the earth bends, and
crouching Atlas can barely hold up the pole around
which the stars are spinning. Outside the Bear, gnawing
at the equinoctial zodiac, Draco follows, with easy
movements of his body, a hissing companion, and
spews against the starry Bull, and all the beasts of the
circle turn in fight against each other; even the planets
collide with each other: Venus bumps against Jupiter,
Mars butts against Saturn; the vernal Pleiades, thrown
out of orbit, approach Mercury who, mixing his light
with the Seven Stars, rises with half his shine next to
his mother Maja, turning himself away from the
heavenly chariot, which he always accompanied." In
the general confusion, which the poet describes in
detail, "all the constellations rise in hostility against
Phaethon until finally the two bears are driven dancing
towards the south and the west. But father Jupiter with
his lightning bolts dashes Phaethon from on high out
of the chariot, into the waters of Eridanus, and
restoring the harmony of the cosmos, he gives back
into the hands of Helios the horses and the chariot.

With the help of rain he then extinguishes the raging fires, and the meadows soon smile again with rich seedlings; as for Phaethon, Jupiter sets him into the heaven as a warning, just as he climbs onto the chariot, and he does the same with the dried up Eridanus, and on its winding banks he sets the Heliades as trees, from whose mourning leaves the precious drops drip into the running stream. Having said all this[125] Mercury returns to heaven, but Dionysos remains in astonishment at the tale of the formerly deranged order of the heavenly bodies, and at the fall of burning Phaethon into the "eventide stream of the Celts"[126] just as his fleet sets ashore, with which he intends to vanquish the Indians." Whether such a general disorder could have affected the solar system at the occasion of the fall of this comet, or whether, more likely, the poet describes them as they would have appeared to the bewildered and easily deceived eye of the beholders, remains for the astronomer to decide.

---

[125] *Ibid.* XXXIX.

[126] "-- πως (Φαεθων) παρα Κελτοις / Εσπεριω πυρικαντος επωλισθησε ρεεθρω , etc"
"

Chapter Seven

The image-tale in Hyginus, Hesiod and Servius.

One image-tale deviating somewhat from the former has been preserved for us by Hyginus.[127] "When Phaethon, son of Sol and Klymene, without his father's knowledge had climbed onto the solar chariot and had lifted himself high above the earth, seized by fear, he fell into the Eridanus. Jupiter then hurled his thunderbolts against him and the world went up in flames. So as not to appear to have destroyed mankind without intending to, Jupiter pretended that he wanted to annihilate it and gathered together all the rivers, and the whole human race disappeared except for Pyrrha and Deucalion who had fled onto Mt Aetna, the highest mountain in Sicily, but Phaethon sisters, who had harnessed the horses without their father's knowledge, were all changed into poplar trees."

An additional version in Hyginus, supposedly lifted out of Hesiod, differs from Ovid's mostly in that Phaethon is given as the son of the ocean-nymph

---

[127] Hyginus, *Fabulae*, 152-154.

Merope and of Klymenus, son of Sol.

According to another version, preserved for us by Servius,[128] and totally in contradiction with all the other legends, it was Eridanus who was the son of Helios who, hit by Jupiter's lightning bolts, fell from heaven, received the name of Phaethon because of his flaming appearance, and gave his former name of Eridanus to the Italian river Po.

---

[128] Maurus Servius Honoratus (fl. end of the 4th century AD), Roman grammarian and commentator on Virgil.

Chapter Eight

Remarks about the date of this event.

In one of the books of Nonnus mentioned earlier[129] the god Dionysos, while threatening him with war, reminds the Indian river god Hydaspes not to pride himself on his relationship with Helios through the nymph Asteria - who was a sister of Latona and the wife of Perseus - and on his grandfather Okeanos. "My father," he says, "hurled Phaethon, the reckless son of Helios, from his chariot, and Hyperion only sighed and did not dare to fight against him; your brother Eridanos was blasted dry by my father's bolts: Okeanos let it be, and did not dare to fight against him. Therefore, spare your waves, so that they should not, like those of Eridanus, be dried up by my fathers bolts."

Considering that our Dionysos was the son of Semele, a daughter of Cadmus, the above indications give a close indication as to the dating of this momentous celestial event. The indications of other

---

[129] Nonnus, *Op. cit.* XXIII.

authors corroborate at this point. Nemesian,[130] in his *Cynegetika* has the fall of Phaethon happening shortly after the arrival of Cadmus in Thebes - Plutarch[131] VIII., p206 ed. Reiske) has, it seems, the Venetians, moving to the Po area only five to ten generations after this event. Even more precise is Orosius, who still held many ancient works before his very eyes, and tells us that around the time that Moses left Egypt there occurred an enduring, severe heat because the sun, having moved out of its orbit, no longer warmed the earth, but burned it[132] so that neither was the Ethiopian able to cope with the heat that he was accustomed to, nor the Scythian able to cope with the heat to which he was unaccustomed, out of which empty minded reasoners had spun together the story of Phaethon. - Clement of Alexandria,[133] who draws together much too closely long periods of time, and sometimes mistakenly conflates different, separate

---

[130] Marcus Aurelius Olympus Nemesianus (fl. ca 283 AD), *Cynegetica* or *On Hunting,*

[131] Mestrius Plutarchus (46 - 127 AD). The Author refers to Vol. VIII. p.206 of the Reiske edition of Plutarch's works of his time.

[132] Paulus Orosius, *Historiae Adversum Paganos,* I., c.10.

[133] Clement of Alexandria, *Stromata,* I.

events, makes Moses, Inachus, Phoroneus and Ogyges
to be nearly contemporaries. Shortly after them follow
Kekrops and Ino, and then in the times of Krotopus
the fire-devastation through Phaethon, and the flood of
Deucalion. Immediately afterwas, he mentions, at the
time of Sthenelus, the rule of Amphictyon, the arrival
of Dardanus in the Peloponese, and the founding of
Dardania through Dardanus, - Syncellus[134] mentions
the second king of Attika, Kranaus, and his daughter
Atthis, for whom the country was first named Atte,
then Attica. In Kranaus' time, the flood of Deucalion
is supposed to have happened in Thessaly, and the
flaring up of Phaethon in Ethiopia. But from Hellen,
son of Deucalion, the Hellenes supposedly got their
name.

According to Eusebius' *Chronikon* the flood of
Deucalion happened in Thessaly, and the fire of
Phaethon in Ethiopia, even before the time of Moses
and the Phoenician Hercules Deuso, 490 years after
Ninus; after those events the plague broke out in many
places.

Those authors, who place the fall of Phaethon
only after these great movements of peoples, obviously
confused the Phaethon we are dealing with with one
occurring much later (as I mentioned before), who,

---

[134] George Syncellus, *Chronicle*.

124

according to Apollodorus, was passed by Tithon falsely as a son of Helios, and who supposedly reigned over Athens as the fifth king after Kekrops.

When we put together the clues and investigations of both old and new authors, it appears from them that the movements of population of Cadmus, Danaus, Dardanus, Moses et al. occurred only after the fall of Phaethon, in the period 1500-1450 BC. We shall be able to determine with precision the actual date of the heavenly event referred to, either when historians succeed in finding pertaining passages of the lost works of Akusilaos and Varro, or when the astronomers manage, by means of retrocalculations, to define the axis change of the earth which occurred at that time.

The high degree of decomposition in which we find palm trees and other vegetal giants when we discover them in the sands of our North points, by itself, only to a very early epoch, but do not precisely to the date of the event.

Chapter Nine

Eridanus in Prussia

Among the old image-tales of the Greeks there
are few that are as comprehensive and beautiful, but
surely none that is as important to our own most
ancient history, than the one of Phaethon. The debris
of this comet fell into the Eridanus, which flowed into
the German Baltic Sea, from where the Greeks and
Romans obtained the precious amber. Already
Herodotus, who made a long sojourn in Italy, had
heard that the Eridanus flowed into the North Sea;
even more decidedly and precisely, the knowledgeable
Pausanias points to the course of this river in the East
of Germany, and additionally reports the remarkable
fact that the statue dedicated to Emperor Augustus at
Olympia is made out of an electrum which is found in
the sandy stretches of the Eridanus, but not out of the
metal of the same name.[135] The poet Nonnus also

---

[135] Pausanias, *Description of Greece*, V. , 12. "--
το δε ηλεκτρον τουτο , ου τω Αυγουστω πεποιηνται την
εικονα , οσον μιν αυτοματον εν του Ηριδανον ταις
ψαμμοις ευρισκεται , σπανιζεται τα μαλιστα , και
ανθρωπον τιμιον πολλων εστιν ενεκα . το δε αλλο
ηλεκτρον ανναμιμιγμεσ εστιν αργυρω χρυσοσ ."

presents us this river, which he classifies under the northern streams, under the name of Keltos. For instance, he has an Indian tell the corpse-laden river of Hydaspes, after King Deriades had killed himself, and Balchus had massacred a great number of Indians: "The Araxes did not rage thus against the Medes, or the Euphrates against the Persians, or the Kydnus against the Cilicians, nor the icy laden Tanais against neighboring Sauromatis, but he often discharged a hail of arrows over the enemy in Colchis; happier than thou is Eridanus, for he preserves in his waves the foreign-born Phaethon, not one of his own peoples, he does not cover with his waters the Galatian, nor did he become a grave to the Kelts, but he rolls from richly dripping trees the amber of the Heliades as a glorious gift to the friendly river-dwellers; the Iberian Rhine carries weapons only against the newborn: as a judge and decider of dubious births, he kills the foreign bastard: but thou [Hydaspes], buries the true children of thy murdered people and does not swallow adulterous blood."

As mentioned before, the poet names the Eridanus, probably in consideration of the origins of the Germans, as a brother of the river Hydaspes. Adding to it the adjective "fire-burned" ("fire-burned brother" - *pyrixauton adelpheon*), probably because, through the fall of debris from the heavenly body, and the following inundation by the sea, the old bed of the

Eridanus became in great part covered up and sanded
over, so that only the small affluent Pregel remained as
an eastward flowing arm of the former, maybe then
westerward flowing river. The legend preserved by
Servius that the Eridanus has its source in the
underworld and then loses itself there again, concurs
with this story, and so does the assertion of Aratus[136]
that this river still exists only as a constellation in the
heavens.

It is true that the Greeks also placed the fall of
Phaethon on the site of the river Po, in Italy, and
Pherekydes,[137] who lived in the time of Cyrus, was one
of the first to identify the Po as the Eridanus[138] but this
happened at the time when the Phokaeans, who got the

---

[136] Aratus (ca 315-310 BC - 240 BC), Macedonian
Greek poet, author of astronomical and meteorological
works. His *Phaenomena* were much translated (including by
Cicero and Germanicus and, later, into Arabic) and are
quoted by Saint Paul (*Acts,* 17:*28).*

[137] Pherekydes of Syros, (6th century BC), Greek
philosopher, possibly a teacher of Pythagoras; *(Of Nature
and the gods).*

[138] As quoted by Hyginus in *Fabulae.* "Hic amnis
(Padus) a Graecis Eridanus dicitur, quem (Padum)
Pherecydes primus (Eridanum) vocavit."

amber from the Henetians, conquered Marseille,[139] and the Celts under Belloves occupied the lands of the Po, and it lasted only until the Senones were chased[140] and the remaining Celts came under the Roman yoke. The Celts had brought the amber trade from the North to this area and this has inspired the delusion among the uninformed that the great celestial event had taken place there.[141] As to the amber deposits, which

---

[139] Note of the Author: As they did not known the country inland at the beginning, they also created the fable, repeated by the commentator of Apollonius, that the Celtic Eridanus divides itself into three arms, of which one (the Rhine) throws itself into the (northern) Ocean, the other (as the Po) into the Ionian sea, and the third (the Rhone) into the Sardinian Sea. *(Schol. Apoll. Rhod.* 1, 4, 596). "Ηριδανος εοτι τῆς Κελτικης ποταμος ; id. 627. Ροδανος , ποταμος τῆς Κελτικης , τω Ηριδανω συμμιγνυμενος , και σχιζομενος , τη μεν εις Ωκεανον φερεται ; τη δε εις τον Ιονιον κολπον ; τη δε , εις το Σαρονιον πελαγος ."

[140] Note of the Author: S. *Kelthenthum,* p 87-88 and 105 - in the first passage the arrival of the Senones I gave too late a date.

[141] Note of the Author: Solinus: (c.20) reports that the Barbarians carried the amber from the north of Germania into Pannonia and Illyria, from where it was brought to the areas south of the Po, which made the Romans believe that it was quarried originated in the forests around this river.

Aristotle calls[142] the amber-islands, the trade with this commodity went directly to Greece. The poets added to this a significant, further element, that the neighboring Henetians, similarly to the nordic Benedians, wore black clothing in mourning for the fall of Phaethon. Diodorus adds,[143] rightly, that the Po had carried for a long time the name of Eridanus.

Strabo dismisses[144] the whole legend of Phaethon and of the amber islands as an empty fable for the sole reason that "the Eridanus cannot be found in the whole world." The fact that this author did not know at all the northeast of Germany has been shown already in my book *Kelthenthum* (p190 and earlier).

Therefore when the Greek poets sometimes give the Rhone, or even some river in Spain, where the Celts found amber or traded it, the name Eridanus, this does not mean in any way, as proposes Adelung,[145] an ignorance of geography, only an always permissible poetic freedom.

---

[142] Aristotle, *On Things heard.*

[143] Diodorus Siculus, *Bibliotheca Historia,* V. c.23.

[144] Strabo, *Geographika,* V.

[145] Adelung, Johann Christoph (1732-1806) German grammarian. *Aelteste Geschichte,* p.9.

Chapter Ten

Boreas and the Eumolpides: the Eridanus in Heaven

Eridanus in Attika got his name similar to the Celtic Eridanos *(Hridano to Keltiko)* from the one in the North because, according to Pausanias,[146] Boreas had abducted there Orithyia, daughter of King Erechtheus, and had married her. Their daughter was Chione. According to Apollodorus[147] she gave to Neptune a son, Eumolpus, from which descended in Attica the priestly family of the Eumolpides, the guardians of the Eleusinian mysteries. Of that same marriage also stemmed the three nordic high priests of Apollo, as we have already related in Chapter 5. But according to the Parian marble chronicle, Eumolpus, son of the Thrakian poet Musaus, had founded the Eleusinian mysteries (in the years 1399-75 BC); and according to Pausanias *(Attica)* King Erechtheus was killed in battle against Eumolpus, together with Eumolpus' son Immarradus.

As the fall of that great comet must have

---

[146] *Op. cit.* Attica. I. c.19, par.6.

[147] Apollodorus, *Bibliotheke,* III., 14, 2,4.

appeared as a whole-world event, it is not surprising
that the Eridanus was admitted among the
constellations.[148] That this happened first with the
Greeks seems to be proven by the name; the Egyptians
called this constellation the Nile, next to which
according, to Eratosthenes, Canopus shone, according
to others, Gyon; the Ganges, in the cosmography of
Aethikus,[149] carried the name Padus (Po).

---

[148] Note of the Author: Bode, in his
introduction to the knowledge of the firmament says:
the river Eridan (a southern constellation) is
represented as a great river with several curves, which
occupies a large area of the sky to the south, below
Taurus, between Orion, the Hare and the Whale. It
starts at the bright star Rigel at the foot of Orion and
snakes towards the West towards the Whale, who
jumps over it. From the whale the river goes again
towards East then south below our horizon so that
its ultimate end, at which a first magnitude star,
Archarnar, is found, is never seen by us...ff

[149] Aethicus Ister, protagonist of a geographic
work written in the VII.-VIII. century by Pseudo-Jerome,
maybe in association with the Canterbury School of
Archbishop Theodore (N. of the T.)

Chapter Eleven

Origin and meaning of the name Eridanus.

To Herodotus the name Eridanus did not appear foreign but Greek, and therefore, to him, suspiscious, yet the good man should have known that his landsmen had a habit of naming many people and places by Greek names, and quite often translated the proper names of foreign individuals into the Greek language.[150] From the Greek, the name could have meant either "the one who burned up in the east," (from *Hri,* East and *danos,* burned) - at least Nonnus refers to the river several times as "the burnt-out" one *(phlekhneis).* Or, it could have meant "the bringer of gifts" (from the old *Hr,* gift, and *daio,* to give, to impart

---

[150] Note of the Author: Plato delivers to us a confirmation of this in *Kritias* when he has Kritias saying: "But before I tell (of Atlantis), I must remind you not to be taken aback when you hear most of the foreign names in Greek. For, as Solon intended to weave these names into his songs, he studied their roots and found that already the Egyptians, the first chroniclers of the above events, had transposed these names into their own language; which is why he also, seizing the etymology of each name, translated it into our own language; and these writings were at my grandfather's and are still with me. *ff.*"

or offer), either because the Eridanus gave to its riverains the precious amber, or because the Hyperboreans conveyed their offerings to Delphic Apollo by using the river Po, from the delta of which they took to the sea near the town of Spina in order to rejoin the island of Delos in the Aegean Sea.

Some moderns derive the name from the Irish and old-gaelic Ire, Eire and Erie, the West so that, reminding one of the Vistula or the Weichsel, it points to its being the westernmost river which, in earliest times, Greek travellers might reach. Others, like Adelung,[151] derive the name from the earlier mentioned Hr, Hri, East and the old nordic Dan, river, which is still found also in Don and Tanais, so that in connection with Germany it designated the Duna (Marcian's[152] Rudon) in the vicinity of which the Estonians gathered their amber. If one wants to add yet more to the possible etymologies, one might advance that this river was named by the Celts Erichdan, or Kings River (from Erich, Erih, hero, king), as Virgil

---

[151] Adelung, Johann Christoph, *Aelteste Geschichte*, p.8.

[152] Marcian, Imperator Caesar Flavius Marcianus Augustus (c.390 - 457), Byzantine emperor from 450 until his death.

had called it the King of Rivers;[153] but one must reflect here that the related Greek Erech-theus is never written with *H (ita),* like Eridanus, but only with *E (epsilon).* The derivation of the first half of the word from the Greek *ρεειν,* to flow, also appears shaky, for that same reason. Quite unlikely on the other hand is the allegation of some authors like Servius[154] about Vergil,[155] that the Po received its name from Phaethon, whose first name had been Eridanos. Suspiscious as well is the passage in the lost work of Cato about the origin of the peoples, that the Po was named Eridanus after the head of a colony of settlers.[156] According to Aelianus[157] there flowed a river of a similar name, the Iretenos, near the city of Itetia not far from Patavia into the Italian Eridanus.

---

[153] Vergil, *Georgics,* I. *"Proluit insano contorquens vortice sylvas/Fluviorum rex Eridanus..."*

[154] Maurus Servius Honoratus (fl. end of IV.th century AD), *Commentary on Virgil.*

[155] Vergil, *Aeneid,* VI., v.659.

[156] "Padus ante a duce Coloniarum Eridanus, sed a profunditate Botigon ab Hetrscis, et Botigum a Liguribus, et a circa arbore picea Gallice Padus appellatur." Theon, commenting on Aratus, calls it "Bochernus."

[157] Claudius Aelianus, *De Natura animalium,* XIV., c.8.

Chapter Twelve

Origin of amber according to the myths of the nordic peoples.

It seems that no specific telling of the breaking up of Phaethon survived as such among the people of our North, but for sure there are some tales about the origin of amber. According to the Edda, it dripped from the world ash-tree, or Ygdrasil, named "Glaser;" a myth from which the Greeks and Romans took the notion that it dripped from the *populus niger* black poplar, or, also, from some kind of fir tree. More remarkable though is an information from Favorinus.[158] According to him, the Celts explained that the Elektrum was not born from the tears of the Heliades, but from those of Apollo when, despondent over the death of Aeskulap, despite the disapproval of his father (Jupiter) he went to the Hyperborean or when, because of the killing of the Cyclops, he was compelled to do forced labor. Where Favorinus, who was able to use for

---

[158] Favorinus Guarinus (1450-1537), Italian lexicographer, author of a vast compilation of Greek authors *Etymologicum magnum sive Thesaurus universae linguae Graecae ex multis variisque autoribus collectus* (1523); he worked mostly in Florence, and was bishop of Nocera.

his dictionary many manuscript pieces now lost to us, found this information is not known; as it is too short in itself, we must also save its interpretation for another place. About the returns of Apollo to the Hyperboreans, see also my *Keltenthum* pp. 10 and 15.

Chapter Thirteen

High value of amber; Elektra walking back towards the North.

As the shattering of this great heavenly body had attracted the attention of all contemporary peoples towards our North, they must also have become attentive to the abundance of amber which now, associated to the stones fallen from heaven, must have appeared to them as a new, almost heavenly product. Whence the great worth which amber found among ancient peoples. (So, for instance, as late as in Julian[159] do the gods throne on golden couches, but Jupiter on a couch of electrum, by which was meant the usual mix of gold and silver, a metal in imitation of amber. Soon after this event, kings and princes gave their gold-haired sons the shiny name of Elektryo, and their daughters the name of Elektra or Elektryone, and only rarely the name Chryseis (Golden One).

The most remarkable is the daughter of Atlas and Pleione, Elektra, with whom Jupiter sired

---

[159] Falvius Claudius Julianus, Emperor Julian the Apostate (331-363 AD), philosopher and writer, *The Caesars*, c.2.

Dardanus who took one part of his people to migrate from Upper Moesia into the Troad. With her six sisters she was placed into the heaven by Jupiter, where they made up the constellation of the Pleiades. But she left her position in sadness over the destruction of Troy and the annihilation of the race of Dardanus. (From the Northwest of Thrace, the Dardanians had moved into Troy whence, after the destruction of the kingdom, one part of them saved itself by returning back north). She isolated herself ever more from the games and dances of her sisters and wandered off with a wildly flowing head of hair towards the North Pole, so that now she appeared to mortals as a comet. She then disappeared, and reappeared from time to time, always with flowing hair and a glowing face, always a foreboding of misfortune to mortals. As, for instance, according to Servius[160] commenting on Vergil's Aeneid, when this red star appears in the form of a brillitant ornament on the helmet of Aeneas and threatens the Celtic king of the Rutulians, Turnus, with imminent defeat. Compare, about this Elektra, the informations given by Eratosthenes, Ovid, Hyginus, Apollodorus, *et al.*

The late Roman women wore the yellowish hair

---

[160] *Aeneid*, X.

of Germanic women as wigs, and Domitius,[161] as reported by Pliny,[162] compared in a poem the hair of his wife Popaea to amber *(succina)*. According to some, the Rhine and the Xanthus, but according to Ovid[163] the Krathis and the Sybaris, made one's hair turn the color of gold and amber.

---

[161] Lucius Domitius Ahenobarbus, known as Emperor Claudius Caesar Augustus Germanicus Nero (37-68 AD).

[162] Pliny the Elder, *Naturalis Historia*, XXXVII., 3.

[163] Ovid, *Metamorphoses*, XV., v.345.

Chapter Fourteen

Names of amber, and their origins.

Finally, we submit here some remarks about the names which amber received among different peoples.

1. *Ambra,* for the French, Italian and English, yellow amber, for amber. *Ambar* and *Ambaron* for the Arabs, *Amber* for the Persians, which is the name of a sweet smelling precious resin, but also of amber. According to Stinner and Eccard, it comes from the ancient German *anbernen,* for "setting fire to." Amber itself is called by modern arabs and Persians *Karabe.*

2. *Bernstein* it is called among the Germans, and in local variants *Börnstein,* in Lower-Saxony *Barnstein,* from the old verb *bernen, barnen,* meaning to burn. In Lesgian (roughly today's Azerbaidjan) *Beri,* and in Lykophron (probably from old-persian) *Perra* are the names of the sun. From which derives, at the time of the Ptolemies in Egypt, *Berenice,* the name of several queens, to which we must add that according to Eustathius[164] (*Odyssee* D.

---

[164] The Author almost certainly refers to Eusthatius of Thessalonica (died 1198), archbishop of Thessalonica, said to be the most learned man of his time, author of commentaries on Homer, the most important contribution to Homeric scholarship in the Middle Ages. It

42) *Beroniki* commonly referred to electrum, whence also *Berniki, Vernix,* varnish, *vernix,* in Persian *pirusah* and *firufah,* a lacker made of amber (german *Firnis*).

Remarkable, too, are the homonymous cities, namely: 1) Berenicae in Epirus, built by Pyrrhus the Young; 2) Berenice, in Solinus: Beronice, one of the five cities of Kyrenaica, otherwise called Hesperis or Hesperides, at the extremity of the bay of Kyrene; 3) a city founded by Ptolemy Philadelphus which carried on a heavy trade with India; 4) Berenice Epidires, a city of the Sabeans on the Arabian Gulf, on the promontory of Aethopia, not far from Dere; 5) Berenice Panchrysos, also a city on the Gulf of Arabia, between the two former ones, in the country of the Troglodytes; 6) a well known city in Koilesyria also called Pella, or Butis; 7) another one in Cilicia and 8) a city known only from Stephanus, which was formerly called Chius - all cities which may be known from their rich amber trade. Even at a much later date, a Germanic king managed to make Emperor Nero a gift of 13,000 pounds of amber.

3. *Elektrum,* "Elektron" for the Greeks, who also gave Apollo the byname *Elector,* and named his sister

---

is a vast compilation of commentaries going back to the Alexandrian school, all of which are lost, but for his citations. (Note of the T.)

Elektra. According to Adelung *(Aelteste Geschichte,* s. 5*)* the word is Phoenician, from the arabic *Ilk, Elek,* resin. The Anglo-Saxons, according to the Thesaurus of Schilters, have *Elothr,* deriving either from the above *Electrum,* or from the old-Nordic *Elldur, Illdur,* fire, and related to the Greek *eilo,* I radiate, shine, and *Eili,* the sunlight, radiating. The *alectorius lapis* in Solinus[165] is probably only a corrupted form of Electrum.

4) *Sentar, Jantar* in old-Prussian, *Jentar* in Russian, *Gyantar* in Hungarian, in fact a lighter, from the local German, still used in Franconia and Bavaria - *kenten, ankenten,* meaning to light, set alight, to which belongs the english to kindle, and our own *Kien,* a match. The fact that the Arabs also name it *Kinthar* becomes more explainable when one knows that Arab coins are often found along the coast of Prussia.[166] (See for the latter Tychens' study of the arabic coins, so common in the regions of the Baltic, in the *Repertorium für Biblische und Orientalische Literatur,* Vol. 3, p. 382-95 - Leipzig, 1780).

5) *Gläsum, Glesum, Glessum,* on the authority of Pliny and Solinus, among the inhabitants of the northern coast of Germany; *Gläsisvol,* in the Edda, is the land of

---

[165] Gaius Julis Solinus, *De mirabilibus mundi,* I., par. 71.

[166] We must bear in mind that for the author, the coast of "Prussia" would have included the East coast of the Baltic as far as Kaliningrad (then Koenigsberg).

amber, and *Gläser* the ash-tree Yggdrasil; originally one
and the same thing as our *Glas,* (glass) old-prussian
Glasso, Estonian *Laas,* from *gleißen,* to coruscate, shine,
from which the old *Glast* for shine, and *Glastum* for
pasture, icelandic *Glasungur* for an icy surface, *Glacies,*
and Low-Saxon *glisseken* for skating on ice (French
glisser...) Greek *ialos* signifies glass, crystal, also, for the
ancient Greeks, transparent resin, amber... Also related
is the Latin *loser,* resin, pitch, as well as *Lasur,* German
for glazing, varnish. See my *Keltenthum...*

6) *Rav, Rau,* in Danish, whence Raunonia, also Basilea,
the old name of the amber island, about which more in
Keltenthum p.87) From the old-Egyptian *Ra, Rue,* sun,
king - therefore, in fact, sun-stone.

7) *Sakrium,* according to Pliny[167] among the Scythians,
Sakal for the Egyptians, maybe the same as *Schecheleth*
in Moses, related to Syrian *schachal,* to drip, like the latin
Succinum, from *succus* and *sugere,* close to german *siegern,*
sickern, meaning "to trickle."

8) *Som-r,* according to Reinegg,[168] among the Finns -
supposedly from the Arabic Somgh, Sumgh, amber;
Somi-sum'n, is a Finn and *Someletn* is Finland, because

---

[167] Pliny the Elder, *Naturalis Historia,* XXVII., c.3.

[168] Note of the Author: *Historische und
topographische Beschreibung des Kaukasus,* Th.2, Anhang p.
178, *ff.*

the Finns formerly held the amber coast. We leave to others the proof of this assertion.

In Japanese amber is called *Kowa-ku,* in Estonian *Lerre-kiwwi,* sea-stone, which might help explain the word *makabi* with which the Greeks designated the larger pieces in the amber trade.

The large diffusion of the northern names all the way to the farthest peoples of the South and the East furnishes proof that those people knew our north, and traded with it from the earliest times.

Chapter Fifteen

*Many erroneous explanations of the image-
tale of Phaethon.*

Since the decay of the Greek priestly
communities, which became ever more pronounced
under Roman rule, and the resulting neglect of all the
mysteries, the knowledge of the old historical image-
language died out, so that the events themselves
became soon to be seen as tales, fables, or were given
erroneous interpretations. Lucian[169] already tried to
explain away Phaethon as an astronomer who had
described the path of the sun but who died without
having brought his research to an end and had left his
science in an unfinished state. Some ignorants then
made out of it the fable of Phaethon, according to him.
Others believed that Phaethon had been a king of the
Molossians[170] who had predicted the coming of a great
heat spell from observing the path of the stars and
who, in order to avoid suffering through it, had thrown
himself into the river Po; others again, like Chompré in

---

[169] Lucian of Samosata, *Works,* V.

[170] Plutarch, *Pyrrhus,* c.1.

his *Dictionnaire de la Fable,* offered that some Dithyrambic poet had wanted to describe a great heat spell and had concocted the story that the sun god had entrusted his chariot to his uncouth son. Clement of Alexandria[171] is of the opinion that this fable had only been invented in order to illustrate the consequences of uncontrolled desire and unfettered passion. Lydiatus[172] confuses our Phaethon with one occurring one century later, namely the fifth ruler after Kekrops who, in youthful folly, he tells us, forgot his father advice: "My boy, use the goad sparingly!" and had rapidly been dethroned. The author of a so-called "oldest history of Prussia" says that the Greeks had invented this legend in order to explain the origin of the sun-stone or

electrum from the resin of poplars; Adelung finally[173] takes Phaethon for a Greek merchant who during one of his trips to the amber country drowned in one of the rivers there and whose story was immortalized in

---

[171] Clement of Alexandria, *Stromata,* V.

[172] Note of the Author: in his commentary on the Parian Marble Chronicle.
- Maybe he is referring to one Simon Lydiatus (1658-1713) (Note of the T.)

[173] Adelung, Johann Christoph, *Aelteste Geschichte,* p.8.

poetry. Much closer to nature, Aristotle[174] had already interpreted this image-tale as a rain of fire, and later still Natalis Comes, almost in total agreement with the above indication of Orosius, as an excessive heat which had lasted until October.

About the Cretan Phaethon, different from ours, we have spoken in the second part.

---

[174] Aristotle, *On the Universe*, c.6.

Part 4.

Later events and natural events until the year 1440 BC

Chapter One

Exceptional human migrations since the Great Floods.

Soon after the flood of Ogyges Latona fled from the land of the Hyperboreans to Delos;[175] some time before the second flood, the Egyptian Inachus founded the states of Argos and Sikyon in the Peloponnese; yet after the Deucalian and the Inachian flood, we no longer find separate migrations, but we see a large part of the peoples of Europe, Egypt and Asia moving on their way to find new places of residence. Out of

---

[175] See Part IV., chap. 5

Egypt, Kekrops founds his new kingdom of Athens; similarly, King Sesostris strikes out of Egypt to wage war on the Scythians across the Ister. His rebellious brother Danaus, or according to Nonnus, Danaus, brother of Agenor, King of Sydon, escaped to Argos and his companion Cadmus, son of Agenor, to Thebes. The secessionist priest Osarsiph,[176] later called Moses, left Egypt around that time. Chased by his successor Joshua, part of the Phoenicians fled Palestine and, according to the memorial columns of Tingis, founded Carthage. The Scythians too may well have wandered out of Asia into the North around that time, for according to Herodotus,[177] they counted no more than 1000 years from their first king Targitaos until the invasion of their country by Darius (513 BC). From Thessaly hails Deucalion, with his sons Amphictyon and Hellen, whose (Hellen's) own sons Aeolus, Dorus and Xuthus repopulate the greater part of Greece. We are told in many places about the new arrivals among them, the Pelasgians, or "tillers of the soil," named thus from the slavic *Pole*, field, and the Greek *asxein*, to work. With Deucalion's daughter Melantho, Neptun - i.e. the high priest of Delos, coming from the sea -

---

[176] Flavius Josephus, *Against Apion*, I., *227*.

[177] Herodotus, *History*, IV., c.7.

sired the Delphus. - The sybilline oracles prophesied new neighbors to the Phrygians, and lo and behold, from the north of Thrace arrive the Moesians, who found Mysia right in their vicinity, while Dardanus, coming from Arcadia together with his son Idaeus, and joining in an alliance with Teuker who had arrived from Crete earlier, founds the Kingdom of Troy, also close to the Phrygians' border!

As we have mentioned earlier, before Cadmus, the Greeks used habitually only the old image writing, as a consequence of which all their tellings of the events of these early times are composed in the old image- language. Only from the time of Cadmus on was the Phoenician alphabet slowly introduced to them.

Chapter Two

The last flood under the reign of Dardanus, and the fire on Mount Ida.

When the aforementioned Dardanus, a neighbor and relative of the Macedonian Amathion, migrated to the Phrygian Ida, Jupiter sent, according to

151

Nonnus,[178] a new deluge, which covered the foundations of the world and went high over the highest coastlines, even drowning the as yet never covered back of Thracian Athos. Shortly thereafter Cadmus arrived to the court of Amathion, on a search for Europa, and there married Harmonia, daughter of Venus and Mars. According to Dion of Halicarnassos[179] and others, an inundation had covered the plains of Arcadia, so that the inhabitants had fled to the mountains; suffering famine, Dardanus now set himself wandering, together with his brother Jasius, his son Idaeus and the bulk of the inhabitants of Arcadia, to the island of Samothrace, and from there to Asia Minor, where they joined up with Teuker. It was probably then that, as Plato tells in Kritias, "the formerly so great Athens, together with its mighty fort, in one single night was destroyed by earthquake and flood, and dragged into the depth of the sea." Clement of Alexandria, moreover, places the fiery eruption of

---

[178] Nonnus, *Dionysiaca*, III.

[179] Dion (or Dionysius) of Halicarnassos (54 BC - ca 8 AD), born in Halicarnassos, died in Rome. Greek historian and teacher of rhetoric, author of *Roman Antiquities,* in twenty volumes, in Greek, a history of Rome from the origins to the First Punic War, of which the first eleven volumes have come down to us reasonably complete.

Phyrigian Mount Ida, as well as the invention of iron
by the Idaean Daktyles (Kelmus and Damnaneus) into
the year 73 after the flood of Deucalion, which, if we
follow his own calculations, gives us the year 1441
B.C., whereas the Parian marble chronicle would
situate it in 1432 BC,[180] which suggest that both events
may well have been almost contemporaneous. Some
generations later, there occurred in Greece, according

---

[180] Note of the author: Before then, many
European peoples used only utensils and weapons
made of copper, as did the Americans in ancient
times. Yet, if the building of the Pyramids occurred
earlier, the Egyptian must have known iron even
then, even our own Northern steel; for, according to
Jablonski, this latter is called in their language *Stali*,
and Clement of Alexandria states explicitly: "The
Norope, whom we now call Noriks, are artists in
metals, they have discovered the art of purifying
iron." Noropian peons were present among those
who had gone to war against Troy, according to
Homer. Today still, (according to L.F. Hermann,
about the making of steel, in *Pallas Nord. Beytraege Bd
3, p 354 ff*) the steel of Carinthia, Kraina and Styria
finds its way over the Levant to India and brings
annually a million gulden. The inhabitants of America
and of the South Sea islands knew no iron before the
first arrival of the Europeans - despite the fact that
the latter are descendants of the Malay, who are
related to the Egyptians and their neighbors.

to Diodorus,[181] and especially in Attica, a great drought and infertility.

That Asia Minor, and especially Phrygia, was affected by floods and frequently recurring earthquakes is stated by Strabo and Pliny. Nicholas of Damascus[182] reports that during the Mithridatic wars,[183] after an earthquake, there appeared a great many lakes in different places in the vicinity of Apamea in Phrygia, where none had existed before; that new rivers and springs had surged through clefts in the earth, whereas others had entirely dried up; that even at a very great distance from the sea, salt water had broken over the land in such amounts that it had covered it with crustacians, fish and other sea creatures. As Strabo[184]

---

[181] Diodorus, *Bibliotheca Historia*, IV., c.61.

[182] Nikolaos of Damas, born ca. 64 BC. Historian of Herod the 1st. Author of a *History* in 144 volumes, of which only fragments are still in existence. They were first published in 1804 in Leipzig by Orelli (*Historici Graeci Minores*, I., Par. 1870).

[183] The three wars between Mithridates VI, King of Pontus, and the Roman Republic took place between 88 BC and 63 BC.

[184] Strabo, *Geographica*, XI.

reports, commenting on Poseidonius,[185] in this
earthquake a great number of cities and over 2000
villages were wiped from the surface of the earth. "In
no other country in the whole world," says Solinus,[186]
"have there occurred such long lasting earthquakes and
subsidences as in Asia Minor; still in the times of
emperor Tiberius, twelve cities collapsed in one fell
swoop."

It must be remarked that Nonnus[187] names the
Dardanian
flood as the third, while completely ignoring the
Inachian.

From the youth of Bacchus, son of Semele,
who was a daughter of Cadmus, down to his own time,
i.e. around 444 BC, when he officially started writing
his history, Herodotus[188] reckons 1060 years, which if
adjusted to our own era, bring us to 1504 BC, so that
Cadmus must have flourished even earlier. According
to the Parian marble chronicle, Cadmus came to

---

[185] Posidonius of Rhodes (or "of Apamea"), ca
135 BC - 51 BC.

[186] Caius Julius Solinus, *De Mirabilibus Mundi*, c.40.

[187] *Op. cit.*

[188] Herodotus of Halicarnassus, *The Histories*, II.,
c.145.

Thebes in the fifth year of the reign of Amphictyon
and built there the stronghold of Kadmea in the year
1519 BC.

Chapter Three

Comets and the piling up of mountains of water.

Pliny reports[189] that the Aethiopians and Egyptians called a certain kind of knotted or twisted comet, which they considered to be a harbinger of cyclones, after an ancient, cruel king of their land, Typhon;[190] so also did they call a cyclone itself ,[191] which uprooted trees and lifted up the water from rivers and from the sea. The occurrence of some extraordinary cyclones of this type has been sensualised

---

[189] Pliny the Elder, *Naturalis Historia*, II., c.23.

[190] Note of the author: Typhon, the hostile brother and murderer of Osiris, is not unlike the Indian Shiva. The form of the word seems to be Greek, yet Jablonski derives it from the Egyptian Theu, *wind*, and *ph-hou*, evil, harmful; Others derive it from Tihfo, *serpent;* or from *Tyfi, Tofe*, the fifth Egyptian month, in which the Egyptians had to bear the hardships of inundations. In the Malayan language, which has many words in common with Egyptian, *Tufan, Tupan* designates a storm.

[191] *Ibid.* c.45 and Aristotle, *De Mundo*, c.4, par. 408.

by the Greek poets in image-tales about the monstrous
giant Typhon, Typhaon, Typhoeus or Typhos, and
been adorned by them in many ways. In order to
avenge herself on the gods for what they did to the
Titans and the Giants, say Hesiod and Apollodorus,
Earth bore Typhon from Tartarus. He resided in
Cilicia, where it is said that volcanoes once raged. He
was the greatest monster ever born from Earth. Down
to his hips he had a human form; his head rose towards
heaven above the highest mountains, and it touched
the stars; his arms stretched from sunrise to sunset; in
place of fingers, hundred dragons came out of his
hands and around his hips frightful serpents wound
themselves in loops, which raised themselves above his
head and uttered a terrible hissing. His whole body was
covered with feathers, his head was covered with
coarse hair, and his chin with a frightening beard. Out
of his eyes fire struck, like lightning.[192] According to the
scholiast of Aeschylus' *Prometheus* (v. 331) he had a
hundred heads from all wild animals. We will pass over
the otherwise well known descriptions and instead
occupy ourselves with the one of Nonnus, which gives
us closer information about the time of the great
natural events and brings before our eyes the great
transformations more comprehensively.

---

[192] Apollodorus, *Bibliotheke*, I., 6, 3.

Chapter Four

The Giant Typhoeus and his comet.

In the first and second books of his epic poem
already mentioned, the poet Nonnus describes the
attempt made by the giant Typhoeus to topple Jupiter
and to make himself the master of the whole of
Heaven. As Jupiter, having hidden his heavenly
weapons in a rock cave, was whiling the night with
Ploto, later to become the mother of Tantalus, Cilician
Typhoeus stole them, following the counsel of his
mother, Earth, and used them to wage war against
Jupiter and against heaven. Out of his many throats he
hollered with the cries of all wild animals, and the
dragons shooting out of them licked the lion's mane of
his neck and twisted themselves around his bulls-horns;
but the army of his hands he rose high up, surrounding
with flames the foundations of heaven; then he seized
the Little Bear with one hand, and with the other,
reaching for the Pole, he dragged down the Big Bear by
its hair; with another hand he crushed Boötes and with
yet another, he dragged Lucifer onto the scene. In vain
cracked the aetherean whip of Helios, for he even took
fast Aurora, held up the bull, and the half accomplished

season languished timelessly on her horses; through the
nightly serpent hair of his innumerable heads, light
mixed with darkness; but by day he shone like the
Moon, rising together with the sun. But the giant did
not rest; in a renewed attack, he turned from the
North- to the South Pole, and with one long arm
seizing Auriga, he battered the back of Capricorn, the
bringer of hailstones, and pulling the two Fish from the
air into the sea, he battered the Ram, a constellation in
the middle of the sky, which makes the spring day
equal to the night. After that, climbing to the welkin,
the army of his outstretched hands obscured the light
of cloudless aether; in the same time, he shook his
army of twitching serpents of which one, early in the
day, crossed through the circle attached to the heavenly
axis, and jumped onto the back of the heavenly
Dragon, whistling mockingly at warlike Mars. But we
must pass up here the massive disturbances and
disruptions which the monster caused in the heavens,
in order to turn our attention to the devastations which
he brought to earth.

Chapter Five

The devastations of Typhoeus on Earth.

Already Typhoeus readies himself for the fight against Jupiter, breaks off and hurls afar the mountain summits of Korykos, he squeezes in one hand the Cilician rivers Tarsos and Kydnos, and chasing the inhabitants of the sea with sharp arrows, he forces them to climb onto rocks and he whips the waves up to the aether; around his hips the sea is now circling, its empty bed he fills with his own body, and his feet are barely wet. He tears off pieces of land to fashion islands, and rolls them into the sea. So the monster goes about, already congratulating himself over the dominion of heaven, so close at hand, while Jupiter, in the shape a bull, still rambles about with Io; yet when Jupiter, reasonably enough, returns to his former shape, and takes notice of his loss, Cadmus, son of Agenor, who had gone away on a search for the ravished Europa, manages to win back Jupiter's weapons through a ruse, with the help of Mercury. Now Jupiter in the heavenly Bull (Taurus) readies himself for a showdown with the monster. On hissing feet of serpents the monster walks over the earth, spews rivers out of his serpent heads, and uproots the mountains of

Cilicia to fling them against the heavenly Bull; walking, he crushes the well-armed animals, the bears, the lions, the dragons, he swallows up all the birds of the air, and first of all the eagle, Zeus' bird; he crushes the ox at the plow, lays to waste the whole cultivated earth, uproots trees and forests, and rolls them far away in front of him; land and rocks he throws into the air, and those make up, by falling back into the sea, the bases for new islands. The shepherds scatter; wailing of Pan, Minerva, of Daphne, of the nightingale and of the swallows over the widespread devastation; Procne, as a swallow, wishes to be one of the Heliades, and shed tears of amber into the waters of all-understanding Eridanus, to bewail her misery.

Chapter Six

His fight against Jupiter and the comet.

Then night broke in over the earth, and Helios
drove the much tossed about chariot through the still
intact Atlantic gates. All the gods fled helplessly to the
Nile, except Jupiter who remained in the constellation
of the Bull. Shooting stars flamed by, impossible to
count, as if chased by a storm, and lightning carved up
the heavens all around; a comet spread its bristly light.
The heavenly rafters flamed up red, burning, and a
colored rainbow spread over the sky. Only the goddess
of victory (Iris, the rainbow) returns to assist Jupiter in
the shape of Latona, showing him the way and arming
her father. Reclining on his couch, the monster had
covered the whole earth and cyclones roared out of his
mouth; and by morning he got up in the shape of a
human being, embraced the world in his thousand
snake arms, and out of his innumerable serpent heads
poured the howling of wolves, the roaring of lions, the
grunting of boars, the hissing of dragons, the growling
of fierce bears and the barking of dogs, in an endless
cacophony. Now the giant threatens Jupiter and all the
gods with annihilation, and to all of nature, promises
chaotic destruction; his missiles are hills, cliffs are his

163

breastplates, rocks are his swords, and rivers absorb for him the blows of the failing lightning. Yet Jupiter hurls the thundering bolts and with clouds protects his own breast against the giant's missiles; but with his army of hands, the giant throws cliffs upon cliffs which by falling back build up mountains, he uproots boulders and piles them up on high, stacks mountain upon mountain until they reach above the clouds; whole forests he throws in the direction of heaven, yet they all fall back, hit by Jupiter's sparks, without damaging anything on earth; he slings rivers up into the heaven with his many arms yet they do not succeed in drowning the lightning of Zeus. Long lasted the terrible battle, for both fighters seemed to be equal in strength. But finally one discharge of Zeus burned up his many hands, another his many shoulder blades; Jupiter's heavenly weapons bashed the skulls of the spotted dragons, the hair of Typhoeus was turned to dust by the coiled comet[193] and this hairy torch being thrown their way, the heads lit up in reflexion; having burned the giant's hair, he seals up the hissing locks with heavenly sparks to bring him to silence; as the dragons die, the poison foaming from their cheeks dries up, and the faces of the giant vanish in sooty smoke; his many

---

[193] Nonnus, *Dionysiaca:* "και πλοκαμουσ, Τυφωνοσ ελιξ αμυθυνε κομητις ," etc.

snowy brows dissolve in white drops, and now he gets
whipped cruelly by all four winds at once; When finally
the giant, mortally hit by lightning, falls down on earth,
victorious Jupiter mocks him as a descendant of
Japetus and an avenger of the Titans in a bitter,
gloating speech, and he rolls over his body the rock-
islands of Cilicia, as an eternal prison. From the
members of Typhoeus cyclones arise, which lash the
waves, and by its writhing frightening earthquakes are
triggered. Thus speaks Nonnus about the matter.

Servius comments about Vergil's *Aeneid* that
the Stoics counted 32 comets, which according to
Plinius originated from the five planets and which he
divided, following Abienus, into six categories. Typhon
belonged to the sixth, having appeared once over
Egypt and once over the northern countries, and had
been seen simultaneously by the Ethiopians and the
Persians, who had suffered all kind of evil and famine
under it. Its color was not of a fiery, but of a bloody
red, its hair lit up only dully, and its sphere was of a
mediocre size and swollen aspect.

Chapter Seven

Additional remarks, and information about Typheus from other writings.

The moving force which triggered the enormous mountain of water which, lifting itself up from the sea, wandered all over the globe, is obviously the Jupiter comet, and one might be surprised that our poet attributes to it only a secondary role, if one did not know that the first Christians, whom Nonnus later joined, trusted Mosaic teachings, which denied all influence to the stars, and negated any changes brought on by them on earth, which they saw ordered solely by divine will. Halley himself has explained the Deluge by the encounter of the earth with a comet, which Lambert denied only because the Almighty in his wisdom had organized the comets orbits so neatly that never should a collision between them be possible. Yet a bodily collision and the mere play of attractive forces are quite different matters.

According to Strabo[194] the event with Typhon was supposed to have occurred in the Land of the

---

[194] Strabo, *Geographica*, XII.

Arimians, i.e. Lydia and Mysia, by the river Meander, a
region which, from high antiquity down to his own
time had often been devastated by earthquakes and by
outbreaks of fire. This event had affected parts of Syria
as well, as a consequence of which, Strabo[195] assures us,
the river Orontes formerly carried the name of
Typhon. Typhon himself, insofar as he is based on
something real, Strabo explains wondrously enough as
a great snake who, in order to avoid the lightning bolts
of Jupiter, had buried deep caves for himself in the
earth, out of which the sources of the river called by its
name had sprung forth; but Diodorus[196] considered
him a gigantic ruler of Phrygia who had been
vanquished there with his companions by Jupiter and
had been killed.

Out of Cilicia, Typhoeus had taken his course
over the mountains of Thrace, heading for Sicily, and
already at the times of Theopompus[197] there raged on

---

[195] *Ibid.* XVI.

[196] Diodorus Siculus, *Bibliotheca Historia*, V., c. 71.

[197] Note of the author: Scymnus Chius,
Orbis Descriptio, v. 369ff.
    Scymnus Chius, or Scymnus of Chios (fl. ca. 185
BC) is the author of a description of the world known as
Periegesis. An anonymous verse *Periegesis*, originally
ascribed to Marcianus of Heraclea, and published in

the Adriatic Sea great twisting storms, much crossed by lightning, named Typhones.

All dangerous storms, plagues, earthquakes and outbreaks of fire, according to the legends of the ancient Greeks, were activated by Typhoeus, trapped under Mount Aetna; but according to the more penetrating and insightful tales of the Iranian Zend Avesta, these evils were caused by the debris of the comet which had been buried deep down into in the innards of the earth by Jupiter.

As children of Typhon and of the Echidna (Otter) the ancients counted: the Hydra, which Hercules killed in the swamps of Lerna; Skylla, whose upper body was of a woman, the lower part of a dog; the Chimaera, a devastating monster in Lykia, an apparition which resembled her father, and whose upper parts were those of a lion, the middle of a goat, the lower of a serpent; Gorgo, as well as others, part real, part imagined monster-shapes, the origin of which one was unable to express otherwise then by the means of the image-language of the times. Solinus[198] explains

---

Augsburg in 1600, was long thought to be the lost work of Scymnus, but this was shown not to be the case by Meineke (1846), and the author is now usually known as Pseudo-Scymnus. *Note of the Translator.*

[198] Caius Julius Solinus, *De Mirabilibus Mundi*, c.39.

the Chimaera as a volcano in Lydia which, Vesuvius
and Aetna alike, sent forth clouds of smoke with
nightly roaring, and had thus given rise to the
aforementioned legend.

Some information about outbreaks of fire and
earthquakes in early times in Sicily, Southern Italy and
the neighboring islands, which, Strabo insists[199] are
related to the fable of Typhon, may be found in the
work of same author.

If in the earliest stages of the shaping of the
earth, typhonic wandering mountains of water may
have been has frequent as had been the volcanoes,
formerly spread all over the earth, the innumerable
leftovers from the sea bottoms, which can be found in
enormous quantities on the top of the highest
mountains, can find in them an adequate explanation.

---

[199] Strabo, *Geographica*, V.

Part Five and Last

Looking back on the events aforementioned

Chapter One

Twice a change of the Earth axis.

The inclined position of the earth' axis with regards to the poles had already lead ancient Greek scientists to surmise that our planet had been thrust by an external celestial body from its earlier perpendicular position; indeed, Anaxagoras taught that at the beginning the stars had turned perpendicularly in the celestial sphere, so that the poles had been orthogonally exactly above the earth [at the zenith of the celestial sphere.] Through the shattering of the two celestial bodies, Hesperus and Phaethon, but especially through the change of orbit of the former, and through the resulting total change in the relations of equilibrium of all the planets in our system, the center of gravity of our earth necessarily had to be displaced, and its earlier position with regards to the poles be changed twice. In fact, the old Egyptian priests, referring to their holy chronicles, which Diodorus and Clement still quote, imparted to Herodotus[200] the following information: "During the time span of 11340 years during which they had conducted observations, Sun had four times not risen at its habitual place, in fact, where he is setting now, he is supposed to have risen twice, and where he is rising now, he set twice. And this had produced no changes at all in Egypt, neither in the fertility of the land, nor in the inundations of the river, nor in the illnesses, nor in the deaths." One confirmation of this is brought to us by Kluegel[201].

---

[200] Herodotus of Halicarnassus, *The Histories,* II., c.142.

[201] Note of the Author: "Ausdehnungen der Erde," [expansions of the earth], in *Astronomische Sammlungen,* III, 164 -69. Malte-Brun, *Abriss der Mathematischen und Physikalschen Geographie,* 1st part (von Zimmermann), p.94.
Note of the Translator: Georg Simon Kluegel (Hamburg, 1739 - Halle, 1812), an innovative German mathematician, made exceptional contributions to trigonometry *(Analytische Trigonometrie.)* Author of a *Dictionary of Mathematics* (unfinished). Conrad Malte-Brun (Thisted, Denmark, 1775 - Paris, 1826) was a French geographer, born in Denmark, author, with Edme Mentelle, of *Géographie Mathématique, Physique et Politique de toutes les parties du Monde,* 1803-1807, in 16 volumes.

This penetrating scholar has in fact found after careful calculations "that all the excellent degree measurements coincide perfectly , and show the earth to be a perfect ellipsoid shape, if only one admits that the original South Pole does not coincide with the actual one, but lies far away from it in the Southern seas, not far from the cap of Good Hope, and that the original North Pole is at the opposite point, in the Pacific Ocean." "Sun, stand still!" called once Joshua, and so it did for one full day, yet this event, which happened only after the time of Phaethon, can be explained more simply having Joshua, according to his own report, vanquish his enemies in a deep valley and chasing them after a hail storm until sunset, then towards evening climbing on the mountain where to the surprise of his gullible bands he still found a high sun and full day, and then continued the battle to the end of the real day and annihilated the enemies.

Chapter Two

Atmospheric transformations on our earth.

The twice violently changed position of the earth with regards to the sun, accompanied by great fires and floods, must also have brought about multiple changes of climate - in part sudden, in part gradual - so that countries which now enjoy a temperate location burned under the hot equatorial belt or froze under ice and snow. As a witness of the times when the hot equator extended over Europe and the high mountains of Asia, the earth of Germany preserves in her lap remains of palms and giant tropical plants, where once elephants, rhinoceros, lions and hundreds of other species of animals of the hot climes thrived; but also of those times, when a deep winter had covered these same regions, so that on the south side of the mountains of Franconia, numberless rests of cave bears have been found, who could only have lived in the cold north. One suddenly falling great winter could with its breath of death have extinguished the southern plants and animals; one, from south coming great flood bury all the northern plants and animals in its deadly waves.

But these sudden transformation we know already from what we have talked about before; about the slower changes, the old-Persian, Greek and Italic poets, from whom the Romans still got their sources, gives us some information in the beautiful and true manner of the image-tale. When king Kronos or Saturn in the West, and Dsjemschid in Aria guided their peoples - so says the legends - the fertile earth, in a perennial spring shining, produced her gifts generously and richly, and the happy peoples lived without worry and pain, without fights and war, through their Golden Age; yet when (after the Ogygian flood) Jupiter had dethroned his father in Crete, a silver era became established, less than gold, but still better than iron; Jupiter shortened the eternal spring, and further parted the year into the burning summers, the icy winters and the unsteady autumns. At that time only did man seek his shelter in caves and huts, tamed the bull, and plowed the land for sowing. To this followed (after Inachus) a third race of men, of a hard spirit, prone to terrible war but not to vice, for it had made instruments and weapons out of copper. Yet since the fall of Phaethon, came the last race, of iron, made greedy by dire want of foreign lands, and able to concieve any act of violence possible. Iron rained from heaven, iron was spewed forth by burning Ida, and the Daktylian

Hercules first fashioned weapons of iron for himself for wars of conquest, but he begged from the Hyperborean Celts of the Ister the symbol of peace, the holy olive tree, in order to crown with it the winners in the Olympic Games. - In an endless war then, North and South battled for the domination of the earth, and the harsh race forged ahead, driven by want and passion, from good to all evil. Already from the height of the Pole eternal ice threatened the green lands of Europa; already the happy lands of the Hyperboreans in the north of Germany were the prey of deep, lasting winters; already the many lions who in Thrace had attacked the camels of Xerxes[202] had disappeared, and the last lions which had roared in the steppes of Skythia[203] had frozen of the cold: yet weaker and weaker became the sound of the enemy clashes, the fire mountains extinguished, waters began to flow controlled by human art, more and more restful becomes the earth and her inclined axis will straighten itself until one day it will be

---

[202] Herodotus of Halicarnassus, *The Histories*, VII., c.124.

[203] Lucian of Samosata, *De Amicitia*, T. VI.

perpendicular again, so that, according to Laplace[204]
the seasons will happen in the same time, and the day
and night all year will be equal in length, and the long
disturbed equilibrium will finally return to our earth.

---

[204] Pierre-Simon, Marquis de Laplace (Beaumont-en-Auge, 1749 - Paris, 1827), *Exposition du Système du Monde,* An IV [1796].

www.ingramcontent.com/pod-product-compliance
Lightning Source LLC
Chambersburg PA
CBHW021104090426
42738CB00006B/500